D1602465

THE GIRL
IN THE
CELLAR

SURVIVING THE HOLOCAUST
IN NAZI-OCCUPIED POLAND

GERDA KREBS SEIFER

Print ISBN: 978-1-54396-704-3

eBook ISBN: 978-1-54396-705-0

For my beloved parents,

Edyta Goliger Krebs and Henryk Krebs

ACKNOWLEDGEMENTS

I would like to thank Professor Bill Younglove for his early help and encouragement in my memoir writing. Over the course of months and years, I sent him emails upon emails of my individual essays. He patiently checked, re-checked, and corrected my mistakes and duplications. I truly appreciate his opinion of my memoir writing, though I feel he has been too generous in his praise.

When Bill taught the history of the Second World War at Millikan High School in Long Beach, he invited me to speak to his class each year. After he retired, our paths crossed again during the planning stages of the Teachers Workshop on the Holocaust at CSULB, along with Professors Jeff Blutinger and Don Schwartz. I learned how intimately he is involved in the study of the Holocaust, the number of meetings he attends, and the many boards he serves on. He knows so much and is so dedicated, and I am sincerely grateful for all he has done for me.

Bill, thank you, thank you, thank you!

To Ellie Brook, who was the first to encourage me to write my story and who is a dear friend. Ellie introduced me to Cecilia Fannon, my editor.

To Cecilia, for helping me see my memoir to completion.

And especially to Harold, for his lifelong and unflagging support.

FOREWORD

I am so very pleased that Gerda Seifer has, at long last, literally, committed to telling her complete story. As many Southern California community members certainly well know, Gerda is a Holocaust survivor. Parts of her extraordinary life have been shared in various books, newspaper accounts, via electronic media, and in various museums. She has also shared with countless audiences over many decades just how she managed to survive the Nazis' attempt to destroy her family's city, home, possessions, livelihoods, and, finally, the members' very lives. She describes here, in great detail, for the first time, the incredible, rich tapestry of home life that her loving parents had created for her— and how the perpetrators, Hitler's henchmen, destroyed her father's business, forced the family into the ghetto, and, ultimately, transported Gerda's loved ones to their deaths. Only Gerda's acquired survival skills, wisdom of her parents, luck via somewhat righteous Gentiles, and incredible perseverance, gave her the opportunity at life beyond the Third Reich's annihilation plan for all Jews.

As Gerda succinctly puts it: One moment she was a Polish girl, one with everything to live for, surrounded by comfort; buttressed by friends, playmates, and classmates, and loved by two adoring parents. In the moments after the September 1, 1939 invasion of Poland, however, Gerda learned, painfully so, that she was, in German parlance, an *Untermensch*—a subhuman without human rights. What should have been her time of physically and mentally growing into adulthood, suddenly became, instead, five long years of fear, doubt, subterfuge, hiding in a cellar, household slavery, and the destruction of both her beloved parents.

Numerous times I have heard Gerda paint a verbal portrait of her mother, particularly. The montage that emerges of smells, foods, songs, dresses, movies, and faces culminate in remembrances, always, of Mamusia. Whether it was obtaining a new doll, a trip taken to outfit her preteen bedroom, a visit to an art show, attending an opera, daily studies at the dining table—or even a reprimand for too childish actions, Gerda shares the love, devotion, and wisdom with which her truly remarkable mother endowed her.

In many respects, Gerda's story is best described by the words "beyond survival." Spared—barely—by the degradation of the camps, but not the ghetto, she lived for some five years on the verge of a captivity that few youths in their teen years will ever have to experience. The unknowns about her parents' own deaths haunted her for years. This book you have picked up to read is the complete tale of Gerda's own odyssey. It has been a lifelong journey, to recover self, seek out those traumatic truths of her interrupted girlhood—and, interwoven—build a life anew in a place, a time, and a country that has, for the most part, valued the talents that those of the Jewish faith and culture have to bring, which are immeasurable. Thanks to people like Gerda, her beliefs—and her tenacity—will assure her own familial descendants, "one moment, a girl or boy"; the next, deservedly so, a world of opportunity.

The University of Southern California Visual Shoah Foundation is creating a hologram of Holocaust survivor testimony. Eventually, we are told, future students will be able to enter a circular auditorium and "meet," and even question, a three-dimensional, projected image of a, perhaps, long-deceased Holocaust, or genocide, survivor telling his or her story.

I remember, however, an afternoon when Gerda, perhaps halfway through her years of such presentations, spoke to my sixth period class at a local high school. One young girl, very much in the dress style of then-popular "punk rock," complete with miniskirt, sleeveless blouse, flaming red—and blue—hair, pierced nose, eyebrows, lips, and tongue, sat in a front row seat, not over six feet from Gerda's chair. What made this teen most distinctive, however, from the rest of her school's small clique, was what was beneath her torn, fishnet leotard stockings that emanated below that miniskirt—all the way to her sandals. Intricately displayed, at two-inch intervals, were carved-in-the-flesh, blue swastikas—at least a dozen visible ones on each leg. Complementing them were an equal number of red swastikas from her wrists to the upper edges of her blouse. During Gerda's talk, the girl stared at her, stonily. Within seconds, however, of Gerda's completed tale, the girl stood up, snatched an awaiting floral tribute from a surprised fellow student's hands, and proceeded to fling her arms around Gerda's neck. Puzzled—and more than a little concerned—I worked my way around to Gerda's back to the chalkboard, to see the girl's face. It was covered with tears. The wetness was already causing her heavy black mascara to run in streams down her face, over the flowers, and, indeed, onto Gerda's own dress. After seemingly interminable moments, the girl abruptly broke her hold and ran out the door and down the hallway.

My concern now? It is mainly this: How will children of the future be able to embrace a hologram? Doing so is elusive. Gerda's presences—and willingness to share, however—have helped create future allies in fighting recurring human atrocities. So, just as the rest of my students have enthusiastically applauded Gerda's sharings over the years, I applaud those readers who have chosen to learn more about her remarkable life, recovered from an evil that, in different disguises, still inhabits, our fragile world.

Bill Younglove
Professor Emeritus
California State University Long Beach

AUTHOR'S NOTE

Some years ago, after telling my story of surviving the Holocaust to Professor Jeff Blutinger's class at Cal State University Long Beach, I had an idea about creating a workshop for junior and senior high school educators to learn in detail about the Nazi genocide so that they, in turn, could teach the subject to their students. Jeff and Professors Don Schwartz and Bill Younglove were enthusiastic about my idea. With their help and seed money from donors such as myself, my husband, Dr. Harold Seifer, Eugene and Eva Schlesinger, and many other generous members of the Long Beach Jewish community, the Trained Endowed Teacher Workshop on the Holocaust began in August 2009. It has been enormously successful with the participants, and I have had the privilege of telling my story every summer since then.

The weeklong workshop reexamines major events that led up to the Holocaust in Europe and addresses the roots of prejudice. Noted historians, guest lecturers, and Holocaust survivors shed light on the causes and effects of anti-Semitism, discrimination, and indifference.

The workshop is dedicated to my parents, Edyta and Henryk Krebs, who perished in the Holocaust.

INTRODUCTION

Forty or more years ago, I was in Israel, traveling on my husband's and my fourth UJA tour. While there, I heard Professor Nechama Tec give a powerful talk on surviving the Holocaust. Nechama came from Lublin in eastern Poland, about one hundred miles from Przemyśl, where I grew up. Our experiences were similar. Something Nechama said that day made me decide to talk to her at the end of her speech, and she encouraged me to write a memoir. Having heard hundreds of horrific stories from other survivors, I never thought my own memories worthy of a book, though I've been speaking about my experiences during the Holocaust for more than half a century.

Nechama is the author of many books and scholarly articles on the Holocaust and has encouraged other survivors to write their own life stories. Since she has a Ph.D. in sociology, she has, in my opinion, a far better grasp on certain issues to write books.

Still, so many Holocaust survivors have published memoirs — some who have doctorate degrees whose English is without blemish, some who are historians, and some who are Holocaust deniers. My own bookshelves are crammed with many of these books. Why should there be another memoir by one more Holocaust survivor?

Friends and students who have heard me speak urge me to write my story. "I'll buy your book," they say. I tell them I'll think about it, turn it over in my mind. Despite their enthusiasm, I wonder who might read it except for my family who already know my story? Then I let the idea rest.

In the early 1960s, some people claimed that only those who were incarcerated in concentration camps were true survivors and that those who merely survived hadn't suffered as much. Was it some kind of competition? Did one earn the title "survivor" by the length and depth of suffering? By what degree do we grade suffering? And when we assign the greatness of suffering, is it an honor to be a survivor?

Nevertheless, Nechama encouraged me to start a book of memoirs without worrying about how to be an author. "Just write," she said. "And when you're done, someone will help you make some sense of all your memoirs." She legitimized for me the idea of writing. Of course, that was a long time ago, and I'm now 91 years of age. My notes have been waiting in the computer for some action for decades.

So I'll begin my story with my earliest memories and see how it progresses.

I have a feeling that some of the events are a bit dim, eight decades on, though other events I remember in great detail. Other incidents are harder to remember, probably having lived during those terrible times under stress, frightened, chased, and forced into hiding. There are blanks in my mind now. Images are fading. It's harder to remember certain people and events, certain smells and tastes. Getting old changes one's outlook, memory, perspective, and even one's voice—I can't carry a tune any longer and I used to love to sing! My voice has become husky. However, when it comes to Russian or Israeli songs, I can still carry a tune fairly well. Maybe American songs from musicals are written in another key.

In writing individual essays, I have come across certain events that after so many years seem unlikely to have happened. I ask myself, "Did it really happen or is it my imagination?" And then just when I think I invented a story, I read the same statement and description from another survivor who went through the same experience as I did, and I realize I didn't imagine these events after all. Some memories were so horrible that it's hard to believe I actually performed certain tasks or ate food I wouldn't dare touch today or performed acts I couldn't have done under normal circumstances. Was it really me, Gerda, who behaved in such manner? No one told me what to do or what to say. How did I know how to act in those situations? I had no one to help me, coach me, encourage me, but I did what I had to do, and my actions helped me to survive.

PREFACE

It was dark and eerie. I sat on a wooden box in a four-by-six cubicle in a chilly cellar in the third largest city in Poland, Lwów. The cellar belonged to an ex-neighbor, the woman who hid me. I didn't dare make any sound in case other tenants would come down to investigate suspicious noises. I could hear people's footsteps outside on the street and occasionally the sound of heavy German soldiers' boots marching by.

It was pitch dark, so I couldn't read or write. All I could do was to sit and think about what was happening in the ghetto. Did Mommy go into hiding as she'd said she would?

Daddy worked outside the ghetto in a factory, making cloth for Nazi uniforms. He had come back one night with news that there would be a large-scale *akcja*, or roundup of Jews, and that people without jobs were going to be "resettled" somewhere else for work. My father had whispered to me to pack a few pieces of clothing because he was sending me into hiding. There was no time for any discussion; I had to obey.

Scared and lonely and helpless, I was utterly dependent on the mercy of the woman hiding me. I kept thinking about my home, my parents, and my old life: the dishes my mother used to prepare, the good times I had on vacations, my school and my friends. It was a carefree life. I realized I'd taken everything for granted up until then.

Day after day, I sat on my little box in a constant state of fear. Hours seemed to last forever. My only contact with the outside world was a quick visit twice a day by the neighbor hiding me. She brought food and emptied my chamber pot, but she brought no news. I felt suspended between life and death, unable to control my life or actions.

CHILDHOOD IN PRZEMYŚL

I was born on August 20, 1927, the only child of Henryk and Edyta Goliger Krebs. My parents named me Gerda, Gerda-Gitle in Yiddish, because they didn't like the name Genia, my grandmother's name. I grew up in the city of Przemyśl on Ulica Marszałka Józefa Piłsudskiego, No. 27, named after the Polish statesmen of the early 20th Century. I lived in that house all through my childhood until February or March of 1940.

The River San runs through the middle of Przemyśl, dividing it in two: the metropolitan area on the east and the suburb on the west, Zasanie. Our city had a picturesque European charm with a lovely park called *Zamek*, or castle, dating from 1842, situated in the hills. I played there as a child, digging in the sand with a bucket and a shovel, swinging on swings, and playing games with other children. Sometimes, I would walk to the top of the park where a tower stood, dating from World War I. In summer, plays were performed on its grounds. I was fascinated by the tower and sometimes imagined that it was haunted. I also had a great respect for it because I could almost visualize the fighting that had taken place in and around it.

In wintertime, I'd pull my sled to the top of the road leading to the park and coast down snow-covered streets. Once during the Russian occupation, a group of us decided to play hooky from school and ski in the park. Though skipping school was naughty and frowned upon, I enjoyed it all the same.

My maternal grandparents built our apartment house in the early 1800s. My parents and I lived on the ground floor in one of the eight apartments, renting out the rest. Ours was the only apartment with hot and cold running water and a built-in bathtub. Across the street from our building, my grandfather, David Goliger, had a lumberyard on the edge of the river San, where fresh-cut logs were transported directly from the river. There, in a large workshop of saws and machinery, logs were cut into boards used in construction. During the holidays when the lumberyard was closed and all the machines were shut down, my cousins and I played hide-and-seek, climbed stacks of logs, and had the run of the place. In summer, I swam in the San and sunbathed on the grass; in winter, when the river froze and the ice became thick, I skated on the river.

In a corner of the lumberyard, my grandfather had built a small synagogue where my father attended high Holy Days services, such as Yom Kippur and Rosh Hashanah. Older men holding prayer books *davened*, reciting prayers, swaying side to side or forward and backward, their heads covered with *tallits,* prayer shawls. At the front of the synagogue was the Aron Kodesh, or Holy Ark, the ornamental cupboard that housed the Torah. A low wall divided the room, and behind the wall were benches for women, an area that always looked sad and lonely to me, as if the little *shul* or synagogue were exclusively the domain of men. That obvious division between men and women began my thinking that certain religious laws were unfair to women.

In spring, as the weather warmed, the ice started melting, and floes glided down the river until all the ice had vanished.

What I remember clearly was the winter of 1939-1940 when the Soviets occupied the eastern part of Przemyśl and the Nazis occupied Zasanie, which means "beyond the San." Hence, the river served as the border between Germany and Soviet Union; the people who lived in the city and suburbs were merely pawns of two occupying nations. Some tried to escape the Nazi occupation by crossing the river at night. They covered themselves with sheets and walked across the icy river to the other side. On some occasions, we were awakened in the middle of the night by a figure or figures shrouded in a sheet, knocking gingerly on our door, and begging us to let them in. We'd give them hot drinks and let them warm up; before daybreak, they would be gone. Sometimes shots rang out, meaning that the border guard had spotted them crossing the river and killed them.

In addition to going to my grandfather's shul, my parents and I also belonged to a large synagogue called The Tempel Synagogue on Jagiellonska Street. My mother and I used to sit upstairs in the balcony where the women prayed. Many women chatted with each other as if they were at a meeting. Since I did not read Hebrew or speak Yiddish, I found the services boring. I'm not sure if my mother read Hebrew, but she always kept her prayer book open and seemed to know how to follow the prayers.

I would look downstairs at the men and try to locate my father among them. Since they were all covered with prayer shawls, it wasn't easy to pick him out.

My family was not very observant, but my father put on phylacteries every morning, little black leather boxes containing parchment inscribed with Torah verses. He'd attach them to his head and turn towards Jerusalem in the corner of the dining room, praying for at least fifteen minutes. My father was a very decent human being and a generous man.

I never heard Yiddish spoken at home, though my parents knew the language. They spoke fluent German since they'd lived under Austrian occupation during the First World War. They used German when they didn't want me to understand their conversation; otherwise, we spoke Polish. It was the Polish language that would save my life during the German occupation, because a Pole with a Yiddish accent would automatically give herself away as a Jew living on false papers.

My parents didn't keep a kosher kitchen nor did they have separate dishes for meat and milk dishes. But we did use a separate set of dishes for *Pesach*, Passover. Our Sabbath candles were sterling silver, eighteen inches tall, decorated with bunches of grapes and leaves. The pair sat atop our dining room cabinet. I used to admire them because they represented something very holy, very special. When the Sabbath candles were lit, I'd watch the glimmer of the burning candles and feel as if I were closer to God. But we lit them only occasionally.

My mother and father were loving, intelligent parents. Mamusia, in particular, was an uncommon lady for her time. She graduated from *Gimnazjum*, high school, an unusual achievement for young women in the early 1900s. My mother spoke fluent German and some French. When I started studying Latin, she checked and corrected my homework, so she was familiar with Latin as well. She knew higher mathematics and a great deal about medicine. My mother was a gourmet cook and baker, an elegant lady, and I was told, admired by many women in Przemyśl. She wanted to study medicine, but in those days, it just wasn't done. On several occasions, my mother travelled to Vienna on her own, once to have a tonsillectomy performed by a famous man, Professor Neuman. He was a well-known physician who'd treated Hitler's mother and who Hitler had wanted as his own doctor. Professor Neuman apparently refused to treat Hitler and left Vienna in 1938. My mother had a picture taken of the professor and his assistants, standing in front of the hospital, long before Hitler came to power.

Mamusia often talked about Vienna, describing the city as full of charm and very elegant. She told me about Prater Luna Park, the oldest amusement park in the world, with its giant Ferris wheel. She also told me about wonderful concerts and operettas she attended at the magnificent Burgtheater in the Ringstrasse, where one hundred fifty years earlier, Mozart's operas had premiered.

My mother was in all respects an amazing lady, a superb example of how I would like to be. Throughout my life, I have tried to come up to her standards, but I have never quite succeeded.

My parents belonged to B'nai B'rith Organization. Once a year, there was a big fundraiser dinner held by this organization, and it was my mother's responsibility to prepare gefilte fish for the entire group.

Shopping and making gefilte fish was a complicated job. My mother went to the fish market in a Jewish section of town. Sometimes I went with her. There she would carefully select large karpie, carp, swimming in huge tubs of water. The fishmonger would then kill the fish she'd selected and gut them for her. We'd often end up at a little ice-cream shop nearby where I was allowed to order any ice cream I wanted or a frozen coffee topped with whipped cream, a special treat.

After getting the fish, my mother would rent huge oval porcelain platters, each one about three to four feet long. Once the carp was cleaned, Mamusia would slice it into serving pieces. The second fish would be ground and mixed with onions, eggs, carrots, and lots of pepper. The mixture would then be stuffed into each slice of the first fish—the meaning, therefore, of the word *gefilte*: stuffed. Each slice was then placed in a long deep pan, head and tail included, covered with sliced onions and carrots, a little bit of sugar, and salted water. After the fish was cooked, my mother would gingerly remove each slice of fish, placing it on a large platter to perfectly form a whole fish. The liquid would then be strained and poured over the fish, forming a delicious jellied sauce after it cooled. The platter was decorated with tiny sprigs of boxwood and blanched almonds, white and pearly. Finally, the gefilte fish would be readied for the meeting at B'nai B'rith, with freshly grated horseradish sauce mixed with cooked beets.

For my birthday, Mommy used to ask me what kind of torte I would like; invariably I asked for hazelnut coffee torte, my favorite, a confection made with layers of ground hazelnuts mixed with butter, sugar, egg yolks, and a little flour. Between the hazelnut layers was a tier of coffee crème, consisting of egg yolks, coffee extract, cream, and sugar. I never tasted the torte anywhere but in my mother's kitchen, and sadly, I never learned the correct recipe and never met anyone who knew how to bake it as well as she did.

My other favorite pastry was kremówki—Napoleons in the United States, *mille-feuilles* in France. Kremówki consisted of many layers of flaky puff pastry interspersed with a middle layer of thick vanilla crème. The whole confection was then dusted with powdered sugar. Some say it was during the reign of Napoleon Bonaparte that the cakes were invented in a Parisian patisserie; others say they originated in Hungary.

Since there was no refrigeration in the pre-war years, kremówki could be made only in winter. Dough had to be placed outside on the windowsill for an hour, then an entire pound of butter was rolled into the dough, and again placed outside to chill another hour. The procedure was repeated three or four times. Only after this process was the pastry baked to form dozens upon dozens of thin, flaky sheets of delicate puff pastry.

One must realize that the stoves in the 1930s did not easily maintain a constant temperature for baking or cooking needs. Only experienced bakers could manage the correct temperatures for various recipes, but my mother had no problem controlling the ovens. With lots of whipping and beating at a low temperature, the crème became thicker, the yolks didn't curdle, and the vanilla mixture was spread between the layers. When the baking was complete, I would sample the heavenly pastries.

One winter's day, new white snow blanketed the streets and the sun shimmered on its surface. I was perhaps three or four years old, bundled up in a scarf, woolen hat, and mittens with a cord attached to each mitten. I was seated on a sled, and my nanny pulled me up the steep hill near the park. We sledded down to the bottom, to Piłsudskiego Street, where we lived.

I loved the feeling of the wind and bits of snow hitting my face as I schussed down. After repeating the run two or three times more, I became fussy. My nanny knew what was wrong so she took me back home, my cheeks rosy from the cold. I was crying. Mamusia knew immediately what was bothering me. She placed a bowl of rosół, chicken soup, in front of her fussy little Gerdusia.

Off came the hat, scarf and mittens, and I was served Mamusia's soup with its round slices of orange carrots and long, delectable, slippery noodles. Oh they were so yummy! My good temper returned in no time, as my mother was certain it would.

My mother was a consistent woman, an admirable trait.

One day, when I was about five or six years of age, I was sitting in my parents' bedroom, looking at myself in the dressing room mirror, making faces, turning my head every which way, smiling, pouting, and posing, as a lot of little girls do.

I was sitting on a red velvet stool, with little pompons hanging all around it. I don't know what came over me, but I took a pair of scissors and began cutting off the pompons, one by one, until they were gone. It suddenly hit me that what I had done was naughty, and I began bawling. My mother came running to the door and asked, "Gerda, what is it? Why are you crying? What has happened?"

"Mommy, Mommy, I'm sorry. Promise you won't be angry with me," I answered through tears.

"I won't be angry," she promised. "Tell me what happened," she said.

I told her then what I'd done, knowing full well that she promised not to punish me. My mother always kept her word. Later, I overheard her talking to someone, saying how clever I had been to extract a promise *not* to be punished before I'd admitted my crime.

I was a Shirley Temple fan when I was seven or eight, having seen every film of hers that was shown in Poland. She was about my age, but the resemblance ended there; my hair was brown and straight while Shirley's was blonde and curly. She was gorgeous—even her name was exotic. She spoke English in films with Polish subtitles and I wondered how she could possibly speak such a beautiful language. Only two words in her films was I able to make out: "yes" and "please." I pored over my collection of Shirley's photographs for hours, admiring every curl, dress, and hat she wore. On occasion, I'd trade a photo for another at school.

One day, I was supposed to see a Shirley Temple movie with a young girl who lived on our street who'd recently lost her parents. Before our date to see the film together, she had to attend a *yahrzeit*, the anniversary of her parents' deaths in the small shul in the lumberyard.

As I waited for her to arrive, I became very impatient that we might be late for the film. I asked Mother, "What's keeping her? Why is she in shul so long? I don't want to be late for the movie."

Mamusia answered, "How can you talk like this? How can you be so selfish? The poor girl lost her parents and she's praying for them…and you're worried about seeing a Shirley Temple film? You will *not* go to the movie at all because you're a very inconsiderate girl!"

I was practically in shock. "Mommy, please! I've got to see this film!" I whined. "Oh, no you won't," my mother responded. I remember dropping to my knees and begging her to change her mind, but her no meant no. I never did see the movie.

On yet another occasion, I called our maid Julia "stupid." Mother overheard me. She scolded me and told me to apologize to Julia for being rude.

"No!" I said, "I won't apologize."

"Well, then, you can go to your room. And don't come out until you're ready to tell her you're sorry." I don't know how long I stayed in my room, crying, but finally I dried my eyes. I knew I had to apologize to Julia because Mommy was right and also because she'd never change her mind. She was resolute and deeply considerate of other people's feelings. She taught me important life lessons and was the greatest influence on my development. I adored everything about her; she was my friend and the best mother anyone could wish for. I knew her to be the best cook and finest baker. She made sure the wood floors were always polished and shiny, that the rooms were bright and sunny. But she wasn't just a homemaker. She introduced me to classical music, great literature, and skiing, among other subjects. She sat with me every afternoon when I did homework, checking my essays, questioning my geography and history lessons. Our house was always filled with fresh flowers. Snowdrops were flowers with dainty white bells sitting atop slender green stems that poked their heads through a carpet of snow in early spring. Mommy would buy them along with aromatic violets and arrange them in vases. We had lilacs in spring, peonies in May, and roses in summer.

I have many memories of golden Polish autumns. In the park, the sky was clear blue, sunlight streaming through branches whose leaves were various shades of gold, red, and brown. Our street was lined with chestnut trees whose dry brown leaves and crunchy outer shells carpeted the ground. I had a rich imagination and would invent games. I used to play with little chestnut balls, sometimes pretending they were loaves of brown bread, which I pretended to sell from a make-believe bakery. I'd explore the small forest on one side of the park, where I'd pick tiny flowers that grew under a blanket of dry leaves. It made me wonder how the flowers were able to breathe, buried under layers of mulch, yet they did. They'd grow in the dark and miraculously bloom, the last plants of the season.

One fall day, my mother woke me gently; it was time for me to get up and get ready for school. She asked me if I'd rather go to school or play hooky and go with her to Lwów to attend *Targi* and *Wystawy*, an international trade fair. It took me a few minutes to make my decision. Imagine having to make a decision about going to the same old school and classes, or go with my adored Mamusia to a large, exciting city I'd never been to before, much larger than Przemśyl!

I dressed quickly.

We were going to see the new furniture on display at the trade show to choose a new bedroom set for me. The trip took about two hours by train. I was overwhelmed by the size of the railway station, by the traffic and crowds and hubbub. I held on tight to my mother's hand.

The exhibition, representing most European countries, was huge. Long halls of exhibitors displayed innovative new furniture, kitchen appliances, china dishes, pots and pans, all manner of house and garden items.

We'd set our sights on bedroom furniture and headed for those exhibits. Both Mamusia and I agreed on a very modern bedroom set of white metal. My bedroom wasn't very large but rather long and somewhat narrow. A large window looked out on the side yard. All the rooms in the house had tiled stoves that reached almost to the ceiling. Opposite the window in my bedroom was a green-tiled stove that provided heat in fall and winter. I enjoyed standing against the stove on chilly days after returning from school or the city, putting one bare foot against a hot tile, pressing my back to other tiles. Then I'd switch feet, tucking the already toasty warm foot into a slipper.

Mamusia ordered the lovely bed frame as well as a mattress, a bedside table, and a table that would serve as a desk. She knew that in a year, when I was a teenager, I would need my privacy.

After we made that important purchase, we went to see an unusual painting exhibit. One canvas spanned the entire circumference of an enormous room, painted by the famous Polish painter, Stanisław Wyspiański. It was a life-sized portrayal of a fight with humans and horses. We had to turn around a few steps at a time to comprehend the whole fighting scene on the colossal circular canvas. I felt as if I were in the midst of the battle, with the horses speeding in all directions, soldiers shooting, using bayonets against enemies, falling off horses, and being trampled. It was a powerful painting, which I believe was hidden during the war. It could have been in the possession of the Russians or the Ukrainians or even the Poles, as Wyspiański was a Polish artist.

The magical day didn't end with the art exhibit. That evening we went to the opera in one of the great opera houses in the world, another first for me. I was amazed by the building, on top of which stood a large sculpture of Glory holding a palm frond.[1] My new dress was velvet and my shoes were rather grown up. Mamusia brought a whole box of chocolates to eat during the performance, a custom in Poland. We sat in a box with red velvet seats. Crystal chandeliers sparkled; they were impressive. I waited excitedly for the curtain to go up and watched all the beautifully dressed ladies and observed the colorful murals, gilded decorations, marble columns, and ornate painted ceiling. All those new and beautiful sights would remain permanently in my memory.

The most disappointing part of the evening was the opera itself, *The Pique Dame*, a gloomy opera about dark passions, obsessive love, and gaming tables. The plot was sophisticated and the music serious, much too hard for a young girl to follow. I wished it had been *Carmen* or *Madame*

---

1   The majestic opera building still stands today, undamaged by war.

Butterfly, music I was familiar with. After a long train ride and a full day in the city, I fell asleep during the performance. Still, that special day spent with Mother engraved itself in my memory.

My father owned a store that had belonged to his father, Pesach Krebs, who was said to have had a sharp sense of humor. One day, a peasant woman from a nearby village brought a live duck to his store to see if she could sell it to one of the storeowners on Franciszkańska Ulica (Francis Street). It happened to be a slow business day, so when the peasant came into his store, asking if he wanted to buy a duck, my grandfather told her that the fowl in question was not a duck but a goose. The woman argued, insisting that it was a duck. While talking with the peasant woman, Grandfather sent his helper to go to others storeowners, telling them to repeat to the woman that she had a goose, not a duck. Eventually, after visiting those other stores, the poor woman returned to my grandfather's store in utter confusion. "Mister," she said, "I thought I brought a duck to town, but now I have a goose. Either I'm crazy or you are."

The Krebs store[2] on Franciszkańska Ulica, Number 8, was one of the most fashionable places to shop in Przemyśl; many elegant stores lined both sides of the street. Daddy felt that with stiff competition among fabric stores, the display window was of the utmost importance, a place to display the newest, most attractive fabrics: silks imported from France, woolens from England, and cottons from Egypt. In other words, the best and latest merchandise available. In pre-war Poland there were no good quality ready-made clothes. People had to buy the fabric to make coats, suits, uniforms, eveningwear, or other attire.

---

2   A few years ago on a trip to Aspen, Harold was browsing in an antique store through maps and historical books. He came across a book on the First World War. He called me over, very excited, showing me a photograph in the book of Austrian soldiers leaving St. Francis church in Przemyśl. "Isn't this the street your father's store was on?" he asked. I took one look at the photograph and a shiver went through me. Not only was it the photo of the street where my father's store stood, but further down that street I noticed a signpost hanging above the store with my grandfather's name on it: "P. Krebs." What a lucky moment! The picture was part of my lost history, and I had so little left of my family's memoirs, letters, or photos. The book was a true find and very meaningful to see my grandfather's name in a history book. Of course, we bought it and copied the photograph for others to see.

Around 1937, our store's window was covered in black paper. Holes were cut in the paper to represent eyes, nose and lips, through which people had to peer in order to see the display inside. The holes suited both tall and short people, drawn to the mysterious window, because they couldn't see anything unless they looked through the cutouts of the eyes, nose, or mouth. The black paper display became the talk of the town for some time.

There were few cars in those days; *dorożki*, horse-drawn carriages, clip-clopped across cobblestones. During the daytime, people loved to window shop on the street. Nighttime drew young people to gossip, discuss daily events, politics, new clothing styles, or just stroll with friends. Often, they'd end up in cafés, having coffee and ice cream, talking for hours. Franciszkańska was also the place to show off their new shoes, suits, hats, and the latest hairstyles.

A few doors up from the Krebs store stood the 18th century Catholic church, St. Francis. Beggars, mostly old, toothless, disfigured women, sat on the lowest step of the church, hands outstretched. On Fridays, the beggars would come to the stores, and each storeowner was expected to give them some money. The beggars were religious about the handouts and never missed a Friday. They knew they could beg on the street anytime, but Friday was a special day for them.

My father was a sweet, good-natured man. He had blue eyes, rosy cheeks, and was bald. I used to call him my sweet "baldy." He told me that he had had blond wavy hair before he had gone into the Austrian army during World War I, and that wearing a helmet caused his hair loss. I don't know if the helmet caused his baldness, but Daddy had a photograph of himself as an Austrian high school student in a sharp uniform and he did, in fact, have wavy blond hair at that time.[3]

My father was a respected merchant with a stylish clientele. He'd studied textiles in Paris before he worked in his father's business.

---

3   Today in my nineties I am pretty thin on top of my head and I never wore a helmet. I blame our loss of hair on our genes.

Each day, the store would remain open until 2:00 p.m., at which time Daddy would come home for dinner, the main meal of the day. He'd rest a bit until 4:00 p.m., then return to work and keep the store open until 7:00 p.m. He was a polite and solicitous salesman. He didn't hurry his customers along or act impatiently, and he was most understanding about payments, about customers changing their minds, or about colors and textures. He had good taste in clothing, knew the quality of fabrics, and always carried the latest merchandise. He was tactful and skillful at making each customer feel comfortable. Daddy worked every day but Sunday; on that day, he liked to play card games like gin rummy with friends at the club. He never played cards at home.

Not only was my father a good businessman but also a very honest man. My mother helped out in the store part-time. Many women knew that she had refined taste and sought her advice in selecting just the right fabric or style for them.

Once I asked my mother how she and my father had met, and she jokingly said, "Well, there was a big long line of men waiting to meet me, and I just picked Daddy." They both grew up in Przemyśl.

I loved my father and was always confident that he'd take care of us under any circumstances, that he'd manage any situation, that he'd rescue us from any difficulty. I had complete faith in him. Once in a while we would have a father-daughter outing. He'd take me for walks on Sunday mornings. As we walked, Daddy would pose mathematical questions that I had to solve. I really enjoyed those questions and tried to solve them quickly to show him how good I was in math. "If you're traveling by train and you leave at such and such time, and the train goes so many miles per hour, how soon would you get to your destination?" It was fun for me and we enjoyed each other's company. In the park Daddy liked to give business to all the little merchant stands that we passed, stands that sold pretzels, halvah, various candies, and chocolates. He made sure to visit every stand. I loved getting all the goodies, but when I got home, I sometimes felt sick from eating too many sweets and snacks; Mamusia would get angry with Daddy for indulging me too much. But I was his little girl and I could do no wrong.

We were a middle-class family. Like most middle-class families in Poland, we had a maid. The maid I remember best was Julia, who lived with us for about seven years until the outbreak of World War II. She came from the countryside, and my mother taught her to cook, polish furniture, buff the parquet floors, vacuum Persian carpets, polish brass knobs, wash windows, and many other household chores. Back then, young women came to the city with little experience and education and learned their skills by working in private homes, including how to prepare meals and serve them properly. The maids went to church on Sunday, their day off. Usually they dated policemen or soldiers. Eventually these maids got married and started their own families. By then, they had learned how to cook and to manage their own houses and children of their own.

I cannot remember where Julia slept while she lived with us. Next to my bedroom was a guest room, although we didn't often have guests. Instead, the room was used annually to store matzos, baked just before *Pesach* and delivered to households in a huge basket to be stored in our guest room a week before the holiday. The matzos were fresh and crisp and round. Often, Daddy would sneak into the guest room to nibble on a fresh matzo, but by the end of the holiday, he'd get tired of eating them, yearning instead for a piece of fresh rye bread. It so happened that Julia was allowed to keep bread in one kitchen drawer during the Passover holiday. Daddy would slip into the kitchen when no one was around and filch a piece of her bread. We all knew what he was doing, but we pretended not to notice.

We had a tradition for Mother's Day. Daddy and I would buy a bouquet of peonies and hide them in our cool cellar, since we had no refrigeration. On the morning of Mother's Day, I'd run to the garden cellar, scoop up the flowers, and present Mamusia with the peonies. She always acted surprised and delighted upon receiving them.

As a family, we didn't vacation together because Daddy felt that the store must be open year-round and that he should be there to oversee things. In his thinking, it wasn't right that three or four employees would run his store without his supervision. It was an old-fashioned, old world idea but also a shame we couldn't enjoy glorious trips together.

Mother and I took summer vacations of four weeks to different health resorts in the Carpathian Mountains. So off we would go to the Carpathians—Rožlucz, Zakopane or Szczawnica—in the south of Poland. These were beautiful areas, with many small hotels, mineral waters, hiking paths, and thermal baths that reputedly had curative properties, especially for lungs and digestive tracks. We walked and hiked a lot, breathed the fine mountain air, took mineral waters, and enjoyed the company of friends.

But in the summer of 1935-36, instead of a trip to the mountains, we went to the Baltic Sea. Just that spring, I'd had a bout with pneumonia that made me miss many days of school. My mother made me drink a lot of hot fluids throughout the day, such as hot tea with lemon and honey or hot milk with whipped egg yolks and honey. On rare occasions, Mamusia would whip egg yolks, sugar, and sweet wine for my sore throat—a delicious treat that worked wonders. I had to stay in bed and found it very boring, especially when I was getting better and stronger. My mother would let me look at lexicons written in German. Although I couldn't read German, the books had interesting pictures, which kept me occupied for several hours. These books were like encyclopedias, very heavy, leather-bound, and kept in a cabinet with framed glass doors; they were to be treated with respect. I tried hard to keep myself occupied by looking at pictures, wondering what the explanations in old German print meant.

One spring, I spent several weeks in bed. I was sick, bored, and miserable. I remember having Banki cups put on my back and even a treatment with leeches, in order to suck the "bad blood" out of my system— quite an ordeal. Though painless, cupping was somewhat scary because I had to lie still during the procedure. My mother was adept at heating each cup with spirits lighted by a match, which she quickly placed on my back. The hot cup would adhere to the skin, and after a while, it would fall off, leaving brown circular marks that faded with time.

Leeches, on the other hand, were black, squishy, worm-like things. They crawled and tickled my back and after a short time, when they had had their fill of blood, they'd fall off. I remember my mother and Aunt Helen sitting by my bed, making sure I didn't wiggle or throw the leeches off my back before they'd worked their magic. They told me all kinds of stories to keep me still; Aunt Helen even promised to give me her gold wristwatch! Of course, I knew she didn't mean I could keep the watch permanently; it wasn't a gift but something to wear on my wrist during treatment to divert me. We thought the treatments were quite effective.

During my long illness, my mother ordered me a "grown-up" pair of custom-made shoes. You couldn't buy ready-made shoes in a style you wanted back then. Shoes had to be crafted by a well-trained shoemaker. When my shoes arrived, they were absolutely gorgeous, made of navy leather with a T-strap and a higher heel. I couldn't wait to wear them to school, parading them in front of my peers. It took a long time before I could return to school; it felt like I'd been away for months but perhaps it lasted only a couple of weeks.

The doctor suggested that we go to bathe in the Baltic Sea, no matter the weather. In this way I might develop an immunity to frequent chest colds and infections. For a young girl in the 1930s, visiting the sea was unusual, as people didn't often travel such great distances for vacations, especially to the Baltic.

I loved the beach with its clean sand and colorful shells that I'd collect at the water's edge. I placed the shells next to my ear, listening for the hum of the sea. I never tired of watching the waves. I loved the long silky seaweed and round jellyfish that swam with the waves, carried back and forth by the tide. Long squiggly eels washed up on the beach, looking kind of icky, but after they'd been smoked, they were delicious to eat.

Another Baltic treasure was amber, formed millions of years ago from pine trees that exuded sticky resin, entrapping insects, leaves, seeds, and feathers. Over time, water flooded these areas, compressing layers upon layers of living things together until they fossilized. It took thousands of years for such processes to occur and eventually, people living near the Baltic and other north seas found chunks of amber washed up on the beaches.

My mother and I took a side trip to Gdańsk-Danzig, an old port town at the mouth of the Vistula River on the Baltic. People spoke both Polish and German in Gdańsk. The city made a powerful impression on me, especially when I saw young men in brown shirts with swastikas around their arms. They acted militaristic, marching all over the city, raising their arms, saying "Heil Hitler." It was an unusual sight in Poland. Gdańsk was a free city, considered more Polish than German at that time, but the Germans were increasing their hold on the city as the German National Socialist Party, the Nazis, won more assembly seats in government.

Hitler had managed to get his foot in the door as early as 1933. Seeing Nazis was frightening; the swastika represented power and in some unexplained way, it also seemed evil. When we returned home from vacation, my mother took over managing the store, and Daddy would go on his own vacation for two weeks, generally to a spa in Czechoslovakia or Austria, such as Marienbad or Carlsbad.

My father suffered from a weight problem, and it was on his spa vacations that he would follow a rigorous program of swimming and exercise as well as a strict diet. He came home looking fit and slimmer, quite proud of his svelte figure. Then as soon as he returned to the store, his stepsister, Berta Oberhard, who lived upstairs in the same building where the store was located, would send him a "second breakfast" of scrambled eggs and a crispy buttered roll. My mother was not really happy about it. She felt that Aunt Berta should not be sending such tempting second breakfasts. On the other hand, my Daddy did not feel comfortable in refusing the maid who brought the food on a tray. Soon enough, the weight he'd lost would go back on... until the next year's vacation.

Our daily routine began with breakfast: coffee, rolls, and homemade jams. Though young, I drank coffee too. On some occasions, my father would eat soft-boiled eggs, depending on what fresh items the farmer from a nearby village might deliver. Daddy was what we called a *Feinschmecker*, German for gourmet. He'd often take a bite of his soft-boiled egg from the egg cup and ask my mother, "Dear, do you think this egg is fresh?" Mother would assure him that the egg had been laid the day before, "Yes, it is very fresh." At about 10:00 a.m., a light second breakfast was served, consisting of a sandwich, a roll with cold cuts or cheese; I took my second breakfast to school as no food was served there. Dinner was our main meal, served around 2 or 3 o'clock in the afternoon. Polish cuisine was quite gourmet, as well prepared as French and German food, but never given the same measure of respect. Soups were often served as the first course. *Chlodnik*, fruit soups, such as strawberry, blueberry, or raspberry, were served in summer. The berries were lightly cooked with sugar and vanilla, then blended with sour cream and served chilled. Since ice was not available, a cool drink of fruit soup really hit the spot on a hot afternoon. In other seasons, vegetable, mushroom-barley, tomato, or chicken (*rosół*) soups were offered.

One particular soup in wintertime rarely mentioned in cookbooks was made with well-blended prunes, served with a freshly boiled potato. It was comfy and satisfying on cold winter days, thick and sweetish with a hint of vanilla. In the evening we had *kolacja*, a supper consisting of a sandwich, soup, or leftovers like vegetables, noodles, kasha, *pierogi*, dumplings, or *paluszki*, fried dumplings, followed by dessert or fruit. Sometimes my mother made the collation, and other times the maid prepared the food.

Friday was washday; Ruzia, our concierge, had a small apartment in our building. In addition to her duties of keeping the stairs clean, the doorknobs shiny, and the windows sparkling, she also washed our laundry once a week.

Washday was quite an undertaking because we had to first heat gallons and gallons of water in a separate laundry room. Laundry was done on a washboard, a laborious job in a time before the modern washing machine. After scrubbing each piece by hand, the laundry would be rinsed in a large tub. It was necessary to boil the white linens in two round huge kettles on the stove, heated by wood or coal that filled the washroom with steam. On washdays, as I entered the corridor to our apartment, I'd be engulfed in a cloud of steam and soap.

The final step was drying, another arduous task, as the laundry was hung outside on a line in the backyard. Some of the pieces were large and heavy. In winter, the laundry was carried up to the attic and hung on lines there; otherwise, it would freeze solid in the cold air outdoors.

My mother's linen cupboard was a picture of neatness and elegance. All the sheets and pillowcases had to be folded evenly, with the fold facing front, all tied with wide pink silk ribbons. The sheets were embroidered with my mother's monogram, the cotton as fine as silk.[4]

Since Ruzia was Catholic, we cooked meatless dinners on Fridays— meat being forbidden to Catholics on Fridays. We usually served *pierogi* stuffed with potatoes, white cheese, and fried onions or, in summer, with blueberries or cherries, sour cream, and powdered sugar, all very delicious. Other washday dishes were *kluski,* noodles, served with farmer's cheese, or kasha with bowtie pasta, soup, bread, and dessert. *Nalesniki*, blintzes, were a summer specialty served with farmer's cheese or filled with fruit. Pasta was made from scratch, mostly eggs, flour, and a pinch of salt. Pasta noodles, once sliced and dried, could last for a long time. If noodles were made with just one egg and water, they had a shorter life. I remember my mother and Julia rolling dough on the table into huge, thin circles. Each circle was rolled up and sliced thin like angel hair or into wider noodles. They were then dried on the table and boiled for the next meal or stored in individual mesh bags for later use.

Markets teemed with freshly picked vegetables in summer: green peas, carrots, kohlrabi, cabbage, asparagus, cauliflower, beets, squash, bib lettuce, radishes, whole cucumbers, and tomatoes. *Poziomki,* wild strawberries, were sweet and flavorful, served with sugar and sour cream. They were picked in the woods and came to market wrapped in a big cabbage leaf or in a small enamel container. No strawberries ever tasted as sweet as *poziomki.*

---

4   Our linen closet would compare favorably to Martha Stewart's displays in this day and age.

Vegetables were stored in the cellar in the winter months to keep them from freezing. Readying vegetables for winter was another special task, repeated each year. The washroom became a second kitchen. There, heads of cabbage were shredded into a large wooden tub for preparing sauerkraut. The cabbage was layered with sliced carrots, cucumbers, dill, dill seeds, garlic, and salt. When the tub was full, it was covered with circular wooden boards that fit inside the barrel. Heavy stones were placed on top of the lid, squashing the cabbage, and the long process of pickling began. It took some time for the cabbage to become sauerkraut, but my mother knew just how to care for it. Cucumbers and green tomatoes would be pickled as well, given the dearth of fresh produce before summer.

Naturally, my mother made her own jam; there was no such thing as store-bought jam. As different fruits ripened and were available in the market, she'd make strawberry, blueberry, sour cherry, and blackberry jams. Later in summer she'd make golden jams of peach and apricot.

I well remember fish being cooked a la Jewish style—*Po Żydowsku*—and served hot. At each dinner Julia would bring the food on a tray to the dining room. We sat at the large dining room table, properly set with a tablecloth, matching napkins, and silverware. Mother served my father first, then me, then Julia, and finally herself. Julia ate her meals in the kitchen. My father was a fast eater, so by the time my mother had a chance to eat, he was often finished, ready for the second course. Mamusia objected to that on occasion, but Daddy was never curbed of the habit.

Once I remember mumbling under my breath that I didn't like the fish I was served and that "I got all the bones." Mother stopped eating and asked me, "Do you really believe I gave you the worst part of the fish?" I realized that it wasn't entirely true because the whole fish was bony. I felt ashamed that I'd grumbled like a spoiled child. I knew that my mother always gave me the best pieces of whatever food we had. Our food was always delicious, fresh, and well prepared. I felt very guilty about my complaint for a long while. Later I apologized to my mother and begged her forgiveness.[5]

In the center of the dining room on an oriental rug was a large table, heavy and black, possibly ebony, surrounded by matching wooden chairs with leather seats. A second cabinet, topped with marble, held my mother's good china as well as a second set of silverware and crystal glassware. On the top stood our beautiful antique sterling candle holders, decorated with flowers and leaves at the base.

In the corner by windows overlooking the street were two huge pots painted in colorful stripes that held philodendron plants, adding contrast to the dark furniture. The walls were painted citron yellow to give the room a sunny appearance during the cloudy winter months. The plants were always green, with new, young leaves emerging and unfurling, eventually climbing to the ceiling.

Next to our dining room was another room with its own entrance, but we had no use for it, and my family sometimes rented it out.

During the Christmas holiday, our maid, Julia, had a little Christmas tree in the kitchen. I loved it because it was like the trees in the shop windows in town, decked out for the season with glass balls and angels, shiny and twinkling. They gave me a feeling of warmth and beauty. In school, both Jewish and Catholic children participated in making tree decorations—long, colorful paper chains, candies, or sugar cubes wrapped in silver tissue paper or clowns made of empty eggshells. We painted the shells, giving them different kinds of faces. Yet I didn't envy Catholic children who had Christmas trees at home; after only two weeks, the trees and the ornaments had to come down.

Julia told me about the feast of St. Nicholas, who came on the night of December 6th through the tiled stoves in each room, leaving gifts for good children. (Santa Claus must have taken lessons from St. Nicholas on how to carry heavy bags of toys through chimneys to distribute them to all

---

5 I have often heard about people in America describing their mothers as poor cooks, whose matzo balls are like stones, vegetables are tasteless and overcooked, and menus are unvarying. None of this was true in my mother's house.

the children.) Julia said that St. Nicholas would come to my house through the chimney or magically through the window. I didn't really believe her stories, but like all children, I liked getting gifts.

On one December 6th, I decided to stay awake to see if St. Nicholas really existed and if he would actually come to my room. It was a very cold night and my window was covered in intricate ice patterns, making it hard to see through. I stayed awake for the longest time, but eventually I must have fallen asleep. During the night I woke up and there, sitting on my nightstand was a gift box! I was curious to know what was inside but decided to wait till morning and fell asleep soon after. The following morning, I tore through the wrappings to discover something that I really wanted. But I never did actually lay eyes on St. Nicholas, so I couldn't say if he was real or if Julia had been the one who'd brought me the gift.

One day in the fall of 1932, my mother took me to St. Hedwig's school, Święta Jadwiga. To keep me from getting nervous, she didn't tell me that I'd be taking a test, but she told me that a teacher would ask me questions and that I should think carefully before giving an answer. My answers must have been satisfactory, because I entered second grade at an age when I should have been in first grade.

School hours were from 8:00 a.m. until 2:00 p.m., six days a week with Sundays off. Subjects in elementary schools were math, writing, the Polish language, art, gymnastics, geography, and history. From the third grade on, I studied Ukrainian. The Ukrainians use the Cyrillic alphabet, and students were obliged to learn it in order to be able to read or write because eastern Poland had a large percentage of Ukrainians. In the first year of *Gimnazjum*, we had to study Latin and another foreign language, such as French, English, or German.

I remember being in love with one of my teachers in elementary school in the third grade. I don't remember what she looked like or which grade she taught, but to me, she was the most beautiful woman I had ever seen, with long fair hair and a sweet face. At the end of school year, she announced that she was leaving our school to teach in another city. I cried when I heard the news. I found out that she would be traveling along my street on her route out of Przemyśl. I sat at the window the whole morning, waiting for her to go by. After a while, I saw a horse-drawn cart with my teacher perched on the high seat next to the driver, her luggage piled behind her. I had such an urge to rush out to kiss and hug her, but of course, I did no such thing. Instead, I wept as the cart passed by.

At St. Hedwig's, an all girls' school, the students wore black poplin coats with white collars over regular dresses, a kind of uniform. Each class had a few Jewish girls and Ukrainians who were Christian Orthodox. The majority of students were Catholic. During the hour devoted to religion, when the priest came into the classroom to teach catechism, Jewish students went to another room to receive religious instruction. I don't remember much about those lessons because I found them very boring. The teacher, typically a young woman or a rather old lady, lacked the imagination or skill to make lectures interesting. Or perhaps they didn't have the proper teaching credentials or knowledge to teach the history of the Jewish people to children, which was too bad because Jewish history spans over 5,000 years and is chockful of exciting facts and stories. In any case, the teacher's rambling didn't stay in my head. I lost focus and gazed through the window to watch birds flying across the blue sky, wishing I could fly away, too.

One day, our Jewish teacher was sick and we weren't permitted to leave the classroom, so we stayed with the Catholic students to attend the catechism lesson. It turned out to be an interesting experience. One of the Jewish students was a religious girl, Laja, who spoke Hebrew. She didn't attend school on Saturday, because it was Shabbat. The priest was well versed in the Old Testament and he also spoke Hebrew. He spent the whole hour talking to Laja, while the rest of us in class sat listening to them. She was a bright girl, perfectly comfortable speaking Hebrew with him, and the Catholic girls were in awe.

In the afternoons, my mother often sat with me at the dining room table, sewing or knitting, as I did homework. She made sure that my essays were written neatly and if my handwriting was sloppy, she'd tear out the page and make me re-write the work from the beginning. She helped me with math, Latin, French, and even sewing when I couldn't figure how to make an old-fashioned pair of pantaloons. In elementary school we were taught how to darn, a skill that would prove handy during the war. Mother also checked my knowledge of history dates, my ability to read maps, and my ability to memorize poems. If I had prepared my homework well, she would allow me to go out and play. As a result, I was always well prepared for the next day. Looking back, I did the homework because I knew it had to be done, memorizing multiplication and division tables, writing essays, reciting poems by heart, remembering historical dates and learning grammar, French, and Ukrainian.

As a little girl and an only child, I used to amuse myself by pretending to be someone else, someone I admired, someone different. I used to talk to myself in a whisper about how I was dressed and what I was doing. I carried on imaginary conversations on many different subjects, arguing with an imaginary girlfriend, sharing jokes, and arranging parties with her. I was very comfortable carrying on such conversations and spent countless happy hours entertaining myself. However, upstairs in our building lived another family with a little girl called Lula. She was my best friend and we used to play together for hours and hours. We'd cut out paper dolls from outdated fashion magazines from my father's store—two families of dolls, one family for each of us. We invented many paper doll siblings (we were both only children) and wove interactions between the families. We never tired of this game and we never argued. I'd go upstairs to her apartment or she'd come down to ours, where we'd set our families on the windowsill amid lots of paper furniture. Our imaginations were boundless.

I loved those little paper dolls more than real dolls. For one birthday, my parents gave me a doll's bed, made of wood, about three feet long with a proper mattress, coverlet, and linens. In the bed lay a bisque doll, dressed as a little girl from Kraków. I didn't play with her a great deal, but I didn't want to disappoint my parents by admitting that the expensive doll was not my favorite. Lula and I both had porcelain and plastic dolls, but paper dolls were more fun. Our paper children were invariably orphaned and poor; and one was always sick. We gave the dolls lots of problems that they had to overcome. Names were often changed, because we liked so many different names and wanted to use them all. Lula and I always ate a snack while we played; my favorite was a slice of rye bread with butter and a smear of freshly made tomato sauce. I never did find out how my mother made the sauce so delicious and was never able to duplicate her recipe.

I lost touch with Lula when we moved to Lwów, but I always remembered the wonderful friendship we shared and the hours we spent playing with paper dolls.

Most of the time I was a good little girl, but on a few occasions, I stepped out of character. One day when I was about six years old and felt really bored, I decided to amuse myself by knocking on the window, sticking my tongue out at people outside as they passed by. Then I'd quickly duck under the window until they were gone. I repeated this routine several times (what a brave girl I was!). Then I saw an old lady approaching. I knocked at the windowpane, sticking my tongue out at her and ducking. After a few moments with my head down, I returned to the window to see if more victims were approaching. To my horror, the old lady stood directly across from me. I froze. She stuck her tongue out, then her mouth widened into a big grin. I reddened in embarrassment, not expecting an adult to play my stupid game. I found my legs and ran from the window as fast as I could, worried that she would knock on the door to report my behavior. But she didn't. She taught me a lesson I wouldn't forget. I never repeated that silly game again.

I had several cousins. Aunt Berta, my father's half-sister, had two daughters, Irena and Lidka Oberhardt. Though they were only slightly older than I was and lived in Przemyśl, we weren't close. Two other girl cousins were Irena and Lila Goliger, daughters of Samuel Goliger, my mother's oldest brother. Lila was a year or two older than me, and though we went to different schools and lived on opposite ends of town, we saw each other fairly often. Lila, always brimming with ideas, thought of fun games to play. Her older sister, Irena, was far more serious and we were too young for her to play with.

One day Lila thought up a fun game. She suggested we pick sticky, spindly buds that grew on bushes in an empty lot. She suggested we put them in a paper bag, and go to the center of town, taking out one bud at a time and throwing it at someone in front of us. The bud would stick to people's clothing, and not until they sat down would they feel a prickly sensation. What a brilliant idea! I gave her my full approval; after all, I was game for an adventure, especially one that was different and dangerous. "Yes, yes, let's act like two innocent girls taking a walk in the city, window-shopping." Lila cautioned that we must be careful not to draw attention by giggling or laughing when we threw our sticky balls and that we must stay serious. I nodded soberly. Easier said than done for ten and twelve-year-old girls. It didn't take long to fill up each of our bags with sticky balls. We started at na Bramie Square in the center of town, moving onto Franciszkańska Street. That particular day the street was so crowded with pedestrians that two young girls went unnoticed.

We put our hands into the bags, took one ball at a time, throwing it gently at the person walking in front of us. It was quite easy, and no one seemed aware of balls sticking to their clothes. We grew bolder, launching more and more balls at pedestrians, breaking our vow by giggling a lot, but not too loudly. When our bags were finally empty, we walked back to Lila's house for lunch. We felt like warriors returning from battle. Needless to say, we did not tell anyone about our adventure, because we knew we'd be punished. Lila's clever game would remain a secret forever, as we'd never repeat such a daring and successful ambush again.

In Poland, students who wished to advance their studies would enter high school from the sixth grade; those who didn't plan on higher education had to complete seventh grade of elementary school. In Przemyśl, there were several high schools: co-educational Hebrew high school,

Catholic high school run by nuns, co-educational state school, and a girls-only government high school called Szkoła Rządowa. My parents wanted me to go to Rządowa, considered to be the best among city schools. The school was located across the San River, and I had to cross a bridge each morning to get there.

The headmistress was my father's customer, so we had an "in" with her. I had to pass an entrance exam in order to be admitted, but even so, the school did not admit many Jewish students. I passed the exam and was accepted, beginning in September 1938. Of the 150 new students for the first class of *Gimnazjum*, only two of us were Jewish—Anka Peiper, the daughter of an attorney, and myself. I did not sense much anti-Semitism in my class, but sometimes a girl would point out that I was Jewish.

Rządowa was a good experience for me that year, a year that marked the end of my childhood. Later on I realized what an extremely good education I'd received in all the Polish schools I'd attended.

P. Krebs, Gerda's grandfather and father's store in Przemyśl

Gerda at 5 and her mother, Edyta, in the Przemyśl Park

Gerda (left) and cousins Zygmunt and Danusia Shwarzer, 1931

Gerda's cousins, Zygmunt and Richard, in 1933 or 1934

Edyta, Gerda at 7, and cousin Zygmunt

Baltic Sea Vacation with Gerda, Edyta, and friend

Szczawnica in the Carpathians; Gerda, her mother, (right), and friends

Gerda with a friendly bear in Szczawnica in 1934

Gerda in school uniform, starting Gimnazjum in 1938

WORLD WAR II

Hitler had long desired a "corridor" to the Baltic through Poland. First there was the *Anschluss* in 1938, the Third Reich's incorporation of Austria into the German Reich. In March 1939 the Nazis invaded and occupied parts of Czechoslovakia. It was feared that Hitler, with his nonaggression pact with the Soviet Union, would also march into Poland, largely unopposed. Poles and other Europeans desperately wanted to believe that peace could finally be achieved and that Europe would be spared another war. Yet no European country had fully mobilized after the devastation of World War I—with the exception of Germany.

On September 1, 1939, Germany attacked Poland. Two days later, England and France declared war on Germany. Shortly thereafter, the people of Przemyśl awoke to the sounds of what they thought were army maneuvers but were, in fact, German bombs falling. After the third bomb fell, we knew it was for real and we were at war. Massive shelling and bombing came from the air, and tanks and infantry easily overwhelmed Poland's military.

Poland was in total chaos. Tape was applied to windowpanes to prevent glass from shattering and shades were drawn to screen out the light that might attract enemy airplanes from seeking city targets. Many people obtained gas masks and stockpiled food for the cupboard. There was no reliable news on the radio, and no one knew what was happening.

A few days later, I saw Polish soldiers milling aimlessly on the streets with no direction from the top brass. We heard that many of them had fled to England. Stores were closed, food was in short supply, shrapnel whizzed by, and bridges were destroyed.

German spies were everywhere, antiaircraft guns shot blanks, and swarms of people fled, carrying few belongings. My parents discussed the situation and Daddy decided to leave Poland and head east. We didn't think that women and children were threatened, as the Germans were a cultured people, but Jewish men were in danger. So my father decided to leave. We shed many tears, kissed and hugged, and my parents made plans for the many possibilities that might occur in given situations. He left with a knapsack on his back. When he reached the center of Przemyśl, people who knew my father well asked why he was leaving. "Who is going to harm you?" He was a respected citizen who had no enemies in town. After speaking with a few people, he was convinced that it was safe to return home. Of course, my mother and I were very happy with his decision.

In the meantime, the Schwarzers joined us from Jaroslaw: my mother's older sister, Zofia, her husband, Wilhelm, and their son, Zygmunt. The Leibels also came from Bielsko: my mother's youngest sister, Helena, her husband, Henryk, a lawyer, and their eleven-year-old son, Richard, as well as Henryk's parents. Aunt Helena was good-looking and charming, a funny lady with a great personality and an infectious smile. They all moved into vacant apartments in Mother's building.

The "victorious" Nazis entered our town ten or so days after the outbreak of war. Nazi soldiers wore spic-and-span new uniforms and shiny boots, their hair neatly trimmed and cheeks clean-shaven. After all, they did not have to fight in combat but simply conquer Polish cities and lands by bombing them.

A couple of days after Przemyśl was occupied, I happened to be walking to town when I saw a frightening situation. About seven or eight young men were standing against a building, facing a wall with their arms up, while a German policeman, *Schutzpolizei*, pointed a gun at them. I realized at once that the young men were Jewish. I didn't wait to see what happened next and ran home. I breathlessly told my father, "Daddy, Daddy, you have to hide! The Germans are rounding up Jewish men!"

My father quickly hid in the attic that had many nooks and crannies, old furniture, and boxes. Only my mother and I knew he was hidden there. One of us would bring him food when no one was around.

Because the Germans ordered "business as usual," my mother had to keep the store open. When questioned by authority, we all answered that my father, like so many other men, had fled east.

Almost at once the Germans began rounding up Jewish men, claiming they were being taken out for manual labor, such as digging ditches and clearing bombed sites, but these men never returned. In the first ten days of occupation, the Nazis killed about 240 Jewish men. Later, much later, I found out that at the end of two weeks' occupation, the Germans trapped 700 more Jewish men, led them into a nearby forest, and shot them all.

As soon as the Nazis occupied Przemyśl, they immediately placed huge placards with new orders on the main streets of the city; the orders had to be obeyed under the threat of severe punishment. All arms, radios, and bicycles had to be turned into the police. All businesses had to stay open.

A few days after the Germans occupied Przemyśl, a large truck pulled up in front of our store. Since Father was hiding in the attic, Mother was working in the store alone. Three Nazis entered and without any explanation, proceeded to remove the entire inventory from the shelves. Bolts upon bolts of fabrics were taken down and loaded onto the truck. Though frightened, Mother kept her composure, neither protesting nor arguing. After all, she was Jewish, considered subhuman by the Nazis, whereas they thought themselves superior, being "victorious and pure Aryans." It took about three hours for them to empty the whole store; they left with smirks on their faces because yet another Jewish store had been liquidated.

In late September, we awoke to see Russian soldiers on our streets. We knew that Hitler and Stalin had signed a peace treaty in August, but what it really amounted to was divvying up Poland between the USSR and

Germany. In Przemyśl the River San served as the border, splitting our city in two.

Although my father no longer conducted business, he was still considered a capitalist and an enemy of the state.

Our store stopped existing after the Nazis looted our inventory and we were unable to order more fabrics from any European country. A few weeks later, we were awakened in the middle of the night by a loud banging on our door. We jumped out of our beds, frightened at such commotion. To our surprise as we opened the door, three Russian soldiers stood, pointing their rifles at us. They had slanted eyes and looked morose and frightening. One soldier ordered my father to get dressed and took him to the police station. They gave no reason for the arrest and we had no right to ask any questions. In the meantime, the other two soldiers started opening all the closets and drawers, searching for hidden firearms. They found no firearms but helped themselves to our money, jewelry, art, linens, china, sterling silverware, and anything that attracted them. Luxury items were not available in the Soviet Union after the 1918 revolution. All the art, gold, silver, and antiques were stashed away, and ordinary Russians lived a life that included only the basic necessities.

Mother politely requested that they leave us some knives, forks and spoons, but one Russian replied, "Listen, woman! We've eaten with wooden spoons since the Revolution and now it's your turn to eat with wooden spoons." While this was going on, I stayed in my mother's bed, the covers pulled up to my neck. One of the soldiers going through the linen closet said to me quite seriously, "I want to marry you. Why not come with me to Russia?"

"I'm too young to marry," I stammered, "I'm just thirteen."

"Oh, no, you're not too young. I would like to take you with me." My mind raced, trying to find an answer, but I instinctively knew the best course was to keep quiet, not volunteer responses or criticize anything he said, no matter how outlandish. My mother and Aunt Helen were in the dining room, where the third soldier was removing china from a cabinet. Mother had no idea that as her beautiful things were being systematically looted, her daughter was being proposed to by a Russian soldier and that I might be ordered to marry him and move to Russia.

My father was released the next morning from jail. No reason was given for his arrest, but we were overjoyed and grateful that he'd come home.

Both occupying armies commandeered rooms for officers in people's apartments. An NKVD officer occupied one of our rooms. The Russians were very suspicious of Poles, and when they were invited to partake of our meal, they usually refused, fearful the food was poisoned. One morning, "our" Russian officer came into the kitchen, drawn by the smell of browned butter and cooking eggs (still available at that time). Mother offered him eggs, and afterwards, he was so impressed with her culinary ability that he ordered a dozen eggs for breakfast each morning thereafter.

A couple of weeks later, the wife of the Russian officer arrived from Moscow. To our surprise, she came wearing a pair of bedroom slippers, clutching a paper bag that contained all her personal belongings. Average Russians were poor; acquiring such luxuries in Russia required coupons and months of waiting, and even then, the quality of merchandise was shoddy. The officer's wife discovered that she could buy fabrics and shoes in Poland, and soon did so. On several occasions, I saw a soldier standing in the middle of the street with one arm raised, his arm draped with wristwatches. He was having his photo taken to send home in order to brag about owning so many watches. In the USSR, one had to wait six months to a year to get a Russian watch, and there was little choice as to color, type, or originality. A Russian citizen was happy to get any kind of watch after months of waiting.

Some weeks later as I returned home from school, I saw a truck in front of our apartment building, loaded with furniture. As I got closer, I realized it was our furniture, and I wondered why my parents hadn't informed me that we were moving out. Then I noticed a couple of Russian soldiers lifting more furniture into the truck and I shivered, realizing our family wasn't moving at all, but that the Russians were carting away our furniture. Just as the Nazis had taken everything from our store, now the Russians "liberated" us of our personal belongings.

After my father lost his livelihood and all our belongings, my parents decided it was time to leave Przemyśl. It was too dangerous living under the Communist regime as a bourgeois—буржуи in Russian. Those considered enemies of the state, such as professors, lawyers, business people, capitalists, and foreigners, were routinely rounded up in the middle of the night and given little time to pack their belongings. No explanation was given as to why or where they were being "resettled." Doctors were an exception and escaped persecution or exile. The others were loaded onto trains and spent many weeks, journeying deep into Russia to gulags, Russian concentration camps. Sad, frightening stories filtered out of Russia, bewildering stories of children, old people, and able-bodied men who had died from exposure to freezing temperatures, starvation, or disease.

My parents decided to move to Lwów to avoid being sent to Siberia. Daddy obtained illegal documents as a textile worker, having learned how to operate textile machines in France before he took over his father's fabric store. Lwów was a place where no one knew us and therefore could not denounce us to the police. The hope was that my parents would find work as laborers, that I'd attend school, and that somehow we would survive the war by minding our own business. People did survive privation, and my parents were strong, healthy and unafraid of hard work, severe weather, or other hardships. But at that time, being sent to Russia was considered a fate to be avoided at all costs.

We moved to Lwów in the fall of 1940. We had no idea what to expect from the occupation. We were not used to the way the Communist mind worked, and the Russians did not know anything about democracy or capitalism. The Russian people have always been suspicious, but the whole Soviet system was built on distrust and suspicion. People were taught to be leery of friends, neighbors, and relatives. It was imperative that they not discuss anything important with anyone but the closest family. Denouncing and reporting others to the police became an everyday occurrence. People felt helpless and at the mercy of the low characters, who seemed to surface during wartime.

My family felt lucky that we weren't sent to Russian gulags. Though we lost all of our personal property and savings, we were glad to be healthy and together as a family. My father had confidence that he could always make a living and take care of us; we, in turn, were reassured by his conviction.

We found a small apartment and a school for me.[6] My mother got a job in a glove factory, sewing leather gloves. Even though she'd never done such work before, she became proficient at her job and was named one of the top producers in the factory. Indeed, it was a great honor under the Communist régime, where everyone had to meet a certain quota. My father got a job working in a factory, manufacturing cloth for Russian soldiers' uniforms.

We learned to keep to ourselves and never to express our opinion to anyone, to always listen with suspicious ears. We behaved as if it were the best life one could wish for. We realized how very precious freedom was and how easily it could be snatched away.

Life under the occupation was difficult and complicated, not only because we spent so much time queuing for every food staple, but also because we had to be careful of every move and every word we uttered. In order to obtain a ration of bread, a pound of sugar, a bit of oil or soap, we had to stand in line for hours before the store opened. Citizens with their precious food stamps had to stand in line at 4:00 a.m., waiting for the store to open at 8:00 a.m. As the time grew near for the store to open, husky guys pushed their way to the front of the line, elbowing out those more timid and less aggressive. The toughs got their hands on sugar and bread, and the supply quickly ran out. Those who had waited patiently for their rations were told by the store manager that all the food was gone and to try again the next day.

---

6   I was placed in a grade that would be considered 9th or 10th grade in an American
    high school.

I learned certain tricks by forcing my way between the bullies. My parents had to be at work early in the morning and could not be late with a weak excuse like standing in line for bread. The black market flourished, but one could not buy much with money as it had lost its value. The peasants used a barter system to obtain linens, cook pots, shoes, and clothing. The items that the Germans and Russians hadn't already taken were exchanged for meat, bread, butter, or other foods.

The Communists held parades and gatherings to show how happy and grateful people were under Communism and the power of the Soviet Union. It was mandatory for all workers and students to participate in the propaganda show. Those who did not were punished and scrutinized by their superiors, usually Communist Party members. Actually, unless one joined the Party, one could not expect to get a managerial position or a promotion. Most of our friends only had menial jobs because none of them wanted to belong to the Communist Party.

Near our apartment was a lovely little bakery that I passed every morning on the way to school. Each day the display window featured my favorite pastry, kremówki, that cost one ruble apiece. I was tempted to stop in and buy one because I usually had a ruble in my pocket and could have easily afforded it, but I begrudged myself the indulgence. Days and weeks and months went by, and I was tempted each and every day as I passed the bakery, each time checking my desire, promising myself I'd buy one on another day.

June 22, 1941, we awoke to witness a most unusual site: Russians, both soldiers and civilians, were leaving their homes, fleeing what used to be Eastern Poland. They carried the loot they'd accumulated during the one and a half years of occupation. They were literally running, dragging boxes and suitcases with them. We were in the dark about this sudden exodus because we had no radios — it was illegal to own them — and newspapers printed only propaganda. Soon enough we found out that Hitler had "surprised" his allies by invading the Soviet Union early that morning. On the heels of the Russians' flight, we experienced night bombing for the next few weeks during which the city sustained a great deal of damage.

The invasion would be considered a turning point of the war in Europe. Even in Lwów, everything changed. I stopped attending school, the bakery shop closed, and the next day for pastries never arrived. I never had chance to indulge my passion for kremówki. I vowed that one day I'd allow myself to splurge on whatever I craved to make up for the many days when I stinted myself.

On that first day of summer, 1941, the sirens sounded, and people grabbed their children, taking shelter in cellars. There, frightened people prayed, children cried, but most listened for the bombs as they whistled by. We could judge by the sound of the whistling how far away the bombs would fall. Those that hit nearby shook our building like an earthquake. There were times when I was baking bread and an alarm would sound and bombs began falling. I'd ignore the warnings to hide in the cellar; it would be a terrible waste if the precious bread burned. I'd answer, "Yes, I'll be down there in a minute." Instead, I watched the German planes to see if the Russian anti-aircraft guns hit them. Bombings occurred at night and it was easy to spot planes and Russians firing ammunition. Somehow, I trusted my premonition that I'd survive the war. For the same reason, I believed that a bomb wouldn't kill me.

By the time the Germans reached the border of Mother Russia, the unprepared Soviets had had a chance to regroup and reorganize and thus began a long, costly siege that would last months and cause millions of lives.

Russians had many dedicated citizens and Stalin used them like pawns. For Poland, it was a Nazi occupation for the second time. The Germans occupied Lwów again following the Russians' departure. By November, they'd opened a ghetto in the poorest section of Lwów.

Being efficient and precise organizers, the Germans got to work, installing loudspeakers on the corners of main streets that screamed orders all day long, stating that all people had to register (this would give them good information how many people lived in Lwów and where they lived).

Jews received a "J" on their identity cards; Poles had a "P" on theirs or a "D" for *volksdeutsch,* ethnic Germans living outside of Germany.

Everyone had to obtain food coupons. Everyone was made to turn in bicycles, radios, and skis to the police; death awaited anyone who still owned them. The Germans were clever at marketing substitutes for unavailable items. Instead of sugar, one had to use saccharine; instead of coffee, they sold roasted oats. For clothing, they sold paper; I had a paper skirt that looked like real cloth, but I couldn't wash it or it would fall apart in water.

Hitler had planned to reach Moscow before winter set in. But he miscalculated and never conquered Moscow. However, he continued a systematic persecution of Jews, issuing decrees that deprived them of civil rights, even in the so-called German section of Lwów:

- Jews had to wear white armbands with the Star of David embroidered in blue, from the age of 13.

- Jewish children could not go to school because they were considered subhuman.

- Jewish people could not ride streetcars or buses because they were considered subhuman.

- Jews had a curfew and were not allowed on the streets after 5:00 p.m.

The slightest disobedience was punishable by torture or death. No Nazi had to explain to a higher authority why he shot a Jew. When my father left for work in the morning, we didn't know if he'd return home that evening. The Nazis ruled by fear. We never knew what to expect or what might happen the next moment. People disappeared from the streets. Some were loaded onto trains; others were shot for no reason. We were always on tenterhooks. Daddy would come home each day bringing us news that was circulated on the street.

During the darkest moments of the war, when everything seemed lost and it felt impossible to go on one more day, Mamusia would pull a few precious green beans of coffee from a drawer. She roasted them in a pan over a gas flame, ground them, making a pot of wonderful real coffee. As sad and desperate as we all were, the smell of brewing coffee and a few sips of the real brew gave us the courage to continue. The aroma brought memories of better days and helped us cope.

At the start of the war, many people fled from western to eastern Poland, away from the attacking Germans. Russians considered them "foreigners" and thus candidates for "resettlement" to gulags and work camps in Siberia or remote Russian outposts. Many of these people hid or slept in other people's apartments to avoid the NKVD, the Soviet secret police, which always searched for these "dangerous" foreigners in the middle of the night. They'd allow them one half hour to pack their belongings before taking them to the trains. Many of these "guilty" foreigners lived for weeks and months with packed and ready suitcases in case they might be visited by the secret police and sent far, far away to remote parts, deep within Russia. These poor families spent sometimes as much as six weeks on a train in cold and uncomfortable rail cars. In the vast area of the Soviet Union, the trains would go and stop, change directions, switch locomotives and drivers; those who had been rounded up were forced to stay on the train the whole time. They were fed black bread and cold soup.

After weeks of cat and mouse games, hiding and sleeping in different homes so as not to be rounded up as foreigners, Uncle Henryk and his old parents[7] were "found" and resettled to Russia. Aunt Helena and Richard chose to stay with us, hiding each night in different places until my aunt obtained false documents.

One morning, Aunt Helena gathered coupons to go get bread for all of us. By the afternoon, she still hadn't returned home, and we were terribly worried. When my father returned from work, he went to the nearby police station to inquire about her whereabouts. The police reassured him that she had been taken off to some job and that she'd return the next day, not to worry. But she didn't return the next day, or the next, or the day after that. It was the last we saw of her. Richard became part of our family.

---

7 I believe Uncle Henryk's parents died on the long train ride, while Henryk ended up in a labor camp in the Urals.

One day, my parents asked me if I would be brave enough to go on the streetcar to do an errand for them. It was too far for either of my parents to walk and be back home before curfew. And because I did not look Jewish, my parents felt it would be safe for me to travel on a streetcar in their stead.

At fourteen years of age, I felt capable of fooling others and that with a little chutzpah and luck, I could do anything. I told my parents I'd be happy to take care of their errand. Traveling on the streetcar, I didn't wear an armband nor did I take my identification card with me. I behaved as I had before the war. As the streetcar passed a church (and there are many, many churches in Poland) I made the sign of the cross like any good Catholic girl. At the appointed stop, I got off and went to the address my parents had given me. The exact errand is lost in the haze of time, but all went smoothly—no glitches or suspicious glances from the other streetcar passengers. I was quite pleased with my small accomplishment. I got off at my stop feeling satisfied that I could still perform normal, everyday chores and behave as a normal person. As I was walking home, two *Schutzpolizei* approached me. One said to me in German, *"Bist du Jude?"* I was frightened but tried my best to appear calm. I replied innocently, *"Nie rozumię po niemiecku."* I don't understand German. But of course, the meaning of his question was crystal clear. He turned to the other policeman and jokingly said, "Huh, she doesn't understand German." Then in very broken Polish, he asked me again if I was Jewish. This time there was a cold threat in his tone. I had to do some fast thinking because my answer could mean life or death.

I answered calmly, "Yes, I'm Jewish."

"Why then are you not wearing an armband?" he said, his voice sharper. My legs went numb and my mind raced. I had to remain calm and think quickly to give the proper answers. All through the war, in order to protect our safety and in order to survive, I had to try to stay ahead of my enemies and their intentions.

"I'm not quite thirteen yet," I lied.

He looked me up and down, not quite believing me because I was tall even at fourteen.

"And where do you live?"

I had to quickly decide if I should give my real address or make one up. If I made one up and the German decided to go home with me to check my papers, it would spell the end for my parents and me, so I gave him my actual address. He then asked what my father did, and I said he'd had a business that the Russians had taken over. I didn't mention the fact that it has been the Nazis who'd first emptied the store of all inventory at the beginning of the war.

I think the police would have escorted me home if they'd thought they could loot valuables, but I was convincing enough that he believed the Russians had taken everything worth taking. He told me he'd come to our house the following day to check my papers. I behaved calmly and normally, as if being questioned by *Schutzpolizei* was an everyday event. Betraying any nervousness was out of the question. When the Nazis finally let me go, I realized how terribly nervous I had been during the questioning. Though I appeared calm on the outside, my heart seemed to beat in my shoulder.

When I got home, I told my mother what had happened. Then and there we decided that I should go to the school I'd attended during the Russian occupation to ask one of my former teachers to attest to my age. The document might look more like a birth certificate if it were written on school stationery, especially since the Germans could not read or speak Polish well. As it turned out, the teacher was somewhat reluctant to issue this "certificate," saying I was thirteen but eventually gave in. Luckily, the police did not return to check the validity of my papers.

On the outskirts of Lwów near Janowska Street was a sand mountain. Before the war, the sand had been used in construction, but after the Nazi invasion of Poland, sands—*piaski*— were used for a much better purpose, in this case, the murder of Jews. The Nazis were endlessly resourceful in devising new ways to annihilate Jews.

People were rounded up every day on any pretext—walking down the street, for example, or standing in line for food rations. They were ordered to climb into open trucks and were driven to Piaski Mountain. Ukrainian militiamen who had welcomed the German occupiers, sat on each of the four corners of the truck, making sure that victims would not try to escape. The passengers had to keep their heads between their knees so they weren't able to see the direction they were headed. When they arrived at the top of the mountain, they were instructed to get out of the truck, strip naked, and stand at the edge of the ravine, facing the bottom of the mountain. German soldiers would then shoot them in the back and they would roll down the mountain while Ukrainian militiamen covered the bodies with sand to prevent the putrid odor of decomposition. Children were sometimes thrown alive into the ravine, the weight of dead bodies falling on them, suffocating them. The Germans were petrified of infection, especially typhus spread by lice, a disease they believed Jews, in particular, carried.

Stories of such murders circulated in the ghetto, but we didn't want to believe them. They were too preposterous to be true, so we thought of them as wild rumors and denied them. Everyone looked for ways to escape. The problem was how and where to go. No country would accept Jews. Stories circulated about "safe" places, but the sources were doubtful and we believed them to be fictitious.

People who had relatives in foreign countries weren't able to obtain visas for them, and in America, many officials were ordered to delay or curtail the issuing of such visas. There were some righteous officials in different areas who saved many lives by issuing illegal visas, but we were unaware such miracles were happening. In acts of bravery and desperation, some Jews tried going over the Carpathian Mountains to Hungary and later to Italy, a country believed to be safer for Jews. This was risky, since border guards could stop them at any moment, and passage on mountain roads at night was hazardous at best; leaders had to know the way. Unfortunately, many Poles claiming to be the guides would demand outrageous sums from Jewish families, immediately turning them over to German guards for certain execution. There were the intrepid and fortunate few who did succeed in getting over the mountains into other countries, but most of the stories ended in disaster; thus escaping over the mountains ceased to be an option. The Nazis continued to round up people on the streets, but they came to realize it was not the most efficient method of culling Jews, not for efficient Germans.

By November of 1941, all Jews in what used to be eastern Poland were ordered to move into ghettos.

In Lwów, the Nazis ordered Jews to build a high wall that would surround the slums, becoming the Lwów Ghetto. The ghetto was situated in a section of the city that was originally populated by poor Jewish families. Barbed wire and broken glass topped the walls of the ghetto, discouraging escape; armed SS police and their vicious dogs guarded the gates. The ghetto became very crowded with Jews from outlying villages, perhaps more than 100,000.

By the time my family moved to the ghetto, the only available shelter was a greenhouse where farmers once grew vegetables and flowers in winter. It had a dirt floor with neither electricity nor running water and eighteen families lived there already—we were the nineteenth. The glass roof was cracked and we often had to sleep with umbrellas over our beds. We didn't know any families living in the greenhouse and my mother put up a sheet on the roof for a little privacy. There was a single gas burner to cook our meager meals. Daddy had an *Ausweis,* a good "identity" card, because he was a "useful" Jew who helped in the war effort by making fabrics for German army uniforms. My mother, cousin Richard, and I did not have IDs because we didn't have jobs. This was dangerous because the Germans considered us a burden to the Third Reich if we didn't work and, therefore, candidates for extermination.

The German administration required Jews to organize a *Judenrat,* a council of Jewish elders to oversee business, food, sanitation, and other municipal duties within every ghetto in the occupied territories. The Nazis demanded that the council organize a militia of about 500 young Jewish men in Lwów. Almost daily Nazis would demand a certain amount of people for labor detail, which usually meant they were sent to Piaski or to a concentration camp. They also demanded money and jewelry to be brought to the SS Office, and it was up to the militiamen to obtain it. The SS dealt only with the *Judenrat*, not with individual Jews. If the quota of Jews to be "delivered" to the Nazis was not met, members of the *Judenrat* and their families were beaten or executed.

From time to time when I walked outside, the militia would round up Jews to load or unload German trucks. Sometimes I'd be ordered to rid the ghetto streets of dead bodies by loading them onto a cart, hauling them to a section of the ghetto where we'd unload them into mass graves. The corpses included people who had died the previous night, mostly old sick people or starved children whose parents had been deported or murdered. It was a common sight to see emaciated people sitting on the street, leaning against buildings, begging for food. Some people gave bits of food or coins; others had nothing to give.

Each time I was called to work outside the ghetto, I didn't know if I'd return to the greenhouse. Most of the time I stayed inside, though there was nothing to do and no books to read. Few friends visited us in our "new home" nor did we visit them. We didn't want to be seen on the streets of the ghetto. When my father returned from work from "outside," he'd occasionally have news of the wider world or a small treat of food. Before we moved into the ghetto, the Gestapo had offered my father a job as a *Dolmetscher*, an interpreter. He was told that if he took the job, he and his family would remain together and safe. But because he knew that such a job meant he'd have to spy on his own people, he declined. He refused to endanger others in order to save himself. One couldn't trust Nazi promises, and our safety may have lasted only as long as it was convenient for the Gestapo.

Life in the ghetto was dreadful. Lack of cleaning supplies, food, and medicines caused the spread of typhoid fever, lice, and fleas. Bedbugs were everywhere, thriving in our overcrowded, unsanitary conditions.

Every few days, there was another *akcja* of the sick, elderly, orphans, and people who weren't working. They were taken for "resettling." We knew what *akcja* meant: it was a death warrant. Yet we always kept the dream of hope alive, that those who were resettled really did go somewhere else to work, somewhere better, and perhaps a place where there was more food to eat.

There came a time during the summer of 1941 when my father felt it would be safer for me to stay in the countryside. He had heard of a farmer who would let me stay at his farm for a price. My father used the excuse that I had problems with my lungs and that country air was better than city air. Actually, there was nothing wrong with my lungs, but Daddy felt I'd be safer away from the ghetto. Accounts of deportations and shootings increased. Desperation and the sense of being trapped worsened with each passing day.

I didn't have false papers, identifying me as a Christian. In order to fit in on the farm, I tried to behave as one of the farm hands, wearing my hair in braids, a long skirt and a simple, embroidered blouse like other country girls. I was useful in the kitchen and doing chores around the farm. I shelled peas, peeled and chopped vegetables. There was another young woman staying there, one who I was sure was also Jewish, but she and I never broached the subject of religion. I'd go to church every morning, and she would go with me. I was far more familiar with how to behave in church than she was, but I noticed that she copied my every move. When I knelt, she knelt; when I crossed myself, she crossed herself. She never made a mistake and was a quick study. Our conversation was limited to inconsequential subjects. The days passed without problems, though it was clear that neither of us was a natural at farming. We did not look as if we belonged on the farm.

One Sunday evening, a few young people gathered in the farmhouse kitchen. I was joking with a young man, when he suddenly looked at me carefully and said, "You know, you look Jewish." His words were more accusatory than casual, and my blood froze in my veins. Perhaps he was suspicious because I didn't quite look as if I belonged there, that I didn't look like the other peasant girls.

The young man's remark took me by surprise because a moment earlier, we'd been joking and suddenly he was accusing me of being in a forbidden place and having no right to be there. I quickly replied, "You know, my cousin always tells me I look Jewish when he wants to tease me. That really makes me mad!" The young man appeared taken aback, probably expecting a flat out denial that I was Jewish. I pivoted to another subject, but the conversation evaporated, and the evening came to an end.

All night I lay awake, worried that despite not admitting to being Jewish, I may have given him reason to think otherwise. He might call the police the next morning to be absolutely sure that I was telling the truth.

As soon as I could, I phoned Daddy the next morning and told him I had a cold—the code we'd worked out if I sensed danger. He told me to board a train as soon as possible and return to the ghetto. My "safe" place in the country did not last very long.

All through the war, people had to make such sudden decisions, not knowing whether they were right or wrong. If you were lucky, you were right and stayed alive; if you were wrong, you died. Making any decision, even the smallest, was cause for great anguish. My reply to the young man in the farm kitchen was quick and smart. I don't know exactly why I answered in such a manner, but I knew that denying his statement would have been the wrong move.

On an evening in July, my father returned from work to tell us that there was going to be a huge *akcja* in the ghetto. He arranged a hiding place for me in an Aryan area of Lwów. In Poland, those who hid Jews or even helped them by giving them water or some food were punished by death. Those who were caught would be strung up, cords around their necks, swaying in the breeze on the streets. It was a very effective way to discourage other Poles from helping or hiding Jews. In other countries like France, Denmark, or Hungary, those who aided Jews were jailed, but in Poland they were killed. However, we had known a Polish woman and former neighbor before we moved to the ghetto, who promised to hide me for the duration of the *akcja*. Of course, my father paid her in advance. All apartment buildings had cellars that were divided into cubicles used for winter storage: vegetables and heating fuels like wood or coal. Each family and each apartment had its own cubicle.

There was no time for discussion with Daddy. I had to hurry because the Polish woman was waiting for me outside the ghetto walls. I turned to Mamusia, hugged and kissed her, and begged her to hide, too. She promised me she would. One last kiss and I hurried outside into the dark night.

The woman was where Daddy said she'd be. There was no conversation between us; we just walked quickly to her building. She led me to her cellar, a cubicle six feet by four, gave me a wooden box to sit on, and cautioned me not to make noise. She gave me a candle and matches, saying to use them only in an emergency; the light in my cubicle might filter through the boards into another, making any neighbor who came down to the cellar suspicious. It was quite possible one might suspect that a Jew was being hidden.

The woman left a jug of water and a chamber pot and said she'd come in the following morning, bringing food. There was precious little I could do in the cellar. Hours stretched out, lasting forever. I didn't allow myself to think how long I'd have to be cooped up in darkness and cold. Instead, my thoughts centered on my mother, my father, my cousin Richard. How and what were they doing? Had Mother gone into hiding? In the blackness, I had only memories to keep me company. I thought about relatives and where they were now, school friends, vacations, books I'd read, films I'd seen, the wonderful meals my mother used to cook, and the mouthwatering tortes she'd bake for my birthday and holidays. I thought about the high holidays with relatives sitting at our table, eating chicken soup with matzo balls, light as air.

After a while, I ran out of things to think about, and I grew cold. Though initially frightened, I'd become bored, and my fears lessened a little. Above me, just beneath the ceiling, was a small window with a metal cover used for pouring coal into the cellar before the winter months set in. In daytime, the window let in a sliver of light; I heard people walking above, their steps and their voices. I could distinguish women's steps from German soldier's boots. How I longed to see the sun and the sky! My greatest wish was to be able to run barefoot through a field of grass with green blades poking between my toes and the wind blowing gently through my hair. What an innocent and unfulfilled wish it was! Hearing German boots coming closer made me shudder; they could be coming to search the building.

There were many Poles and Ukrainians, who were constantly looking for Jews. The situation on the "outside" changed all the time and was very dangerous. Yes, there were some Poles who were very helpful and generous in their actions, even willing to sacrifice their own lives. Then there were those who were sorry for our lot but were afraid to help Jews in any way. They simply were afraid that they'd be killed. Had I been in their position, I don't know how I would have acted. But there was a third group of Poles and Ukrainians checking faces for "Semitic features," always ready, even eager, to see another Jew murdered. These people did so with such viciousness and satisfaction, often not knowing the person they accused. Sometimes they received a loaf of bread or a bottle of liquor for their "services," but in most cases they reported Jews out of pure hatred.

Hidden in the cellar, days blended with nights, and all sense of time was gone. I seemed to be floating in a kind of Neverland, full of terror and dread and worry for loved ones.

One day I felt I couldn't stay in that black, dank cellar any longer.

I debated the pros and cons of leaving, knowing full well that leaving my prison was dangerous, but I found myself touching the lock, opening the door to the cellar, slowly walking up the steps and out of the long corridor, and then I was on the outside. The sun shone brightly and the sky was a deep blue. My eyes blinked, adjusting to daylight. Suddenly, there I was in the middle of the street, not knowing where to go or what to do; I had no plan in my mind. I was paralyzed. Often, older women would sit by their windows, curious as to what was happening on their street. Lucky for me, none of them looked out their windows that morning, except for the woman who was hiding me. She lived on the ground floor of the building and happened to look out of the window just as I found myself in the street. She ran outside, looked both ways to make sure no one saw her, ran to me, grabbed my arm, and dragged me back inside, hissing under her breath, "What do you think you are doing? Are you crazy? Do you want us both killed?" I remember repeating, "I don't care, I don't care." I had hit a low point.

She pacified me with a cup of tea in her kitchen and convinced me to return downstairs to the very place I'd just escaped. I let her lead me back down the steps to my dank cell.

The next day or so, she came down the cellar steps, nervous and upset. She said the Nazis were combing the area for Jews and that I could no longer hide in her cellar. She was highly agitated.

"Where will I go?" I asked, frightened. I had no options.

She was in quite a state but replied that she'd think of something and return in a little while with a plan.

When I went into hiding, my father gave me a single small diamond wrapped in a kerchief to keep tucked inside my bra so that I could use it as a bribe if I was found. The woman knew about the stone and at that moment she asked me to get it out. "We'll wrap it up like a bandage around your knee for safety so you'll be ready to go when I come for you." Obediently, I gave her the diamond in the handkerchief. She tied it onto my knee and then left the cellar. I felt the handkerchief around my knee. The diamond was gone! I realized that she must have taken it, that she'd only been pretending to help me as a ruse. In the darkness, I swept the dirt floor with my hand but couldn't find the stone.

Later, when she returned to the cellar, she told me she had good news. "The Nazis left the area without searching our street. It's safe for the time being, so you can stay."

In my most innocent voice, I told her that I couldn't find my diamond anywhere. She exhibited no concern when she answered, "It must have fallen out. It's around here somewhere. You'll just have to look more carefully. I'm sure you'll find it."

She then left in a hurry. I thought about the story she'd fabricated about Nazis searching the area. All to get her hands on the diamond. There was little I could do, certainly not challenge her story. My life depended on her hiding me, so I never mentioned the missing stone again. She wasn't satisfied with the money my father had paid her—she had to have the diamond as well.

After six endless weeks, the woman informed me that the *akcja* was over and that my father had sent for me, saying that I could safely return to the ghetto. Happy as I was to leave the cellar, I was nervous walking back to the ghetto. My knees buckled under me as we walked quickly, and I kept asking the woman how my mother was. "Fine," she'd answer. "She's fine." Somehow, her answers rang more hollow each time she replied. My suspicions and alarm grew; I knew something wasn't right, not right at all. At last we arrived at the ghetto.

Daddy wrapped his arms around me in a warm hug. "Where is Mamusia?" I asked, my heart hammering in my chest. Daddy sat me down on the bed, and told me what I most feared to hear. He broke the awful news as gently as he could.

My father had found cousin Richard a hiding place like mine. However, Richard was frightened in the hiding place and run back to the ghetto the next day. My mother had a hiding place for herself but wasn't allowed to take Richard with her. So she had opted to stay with Richard in the ghetto. She had sacrificed her life for him. The Nazis rounded up my mother and Richard days later, as my father stood by helplessly, watching as an SS Commando prodded them out of the ghetto. Daddy would have willingly gone with them, but his decision was to stay alive to take care of me.

He spoke to me with kind concern, but I knew the enormous pain he had to have been feeling. I was feeling it too. Losing my precious mother was the worst thing that had ever happened to me, that worst thing that would ever happen to me.

I froze. I was in shock. I lost time and memory. I can't recall what happened immediately after Daddy told me the horrible news. I remember that he went to work every day, but I can't recall what I did all day in that greenhouse. I know that I remained in the ghetto from the end of August when the *akcja* ended until the end of October 1942.

From all the stories that circulated, my father came to the conclusion that most of the Jews rounded up in July and August—more than 65,000—had been sent directly to Bełżec, an extermination camp in eastern Poland. The Nazis wanted the area to be *Judenrein*, cleansed of Jews.

The remainder of my time in the ghetto is a blank. My father was desperately trying to find another, more permanent hiding place for me. Everyone there urgently searched for ways to escape. My father's work was still necessary for the German war machine, but sooner or later, all Jews would be rounded up.

One day, Daddy spoke to a Jewish woman, who told him that she knew a Polish Catholic woman, Janina Tarasiukowa, who was willing to hide a Jewish girl for a price. Tarasiukowa was afraid to take in the son of the Jewish woman; he could easily be identified as a Jew because he'd been circumcised.

Pani Tarasiuk had four children, including a newborn. Some years before, she'd given birth to an illegitimate daughter who had died in infancy. Had that child lived, she'd have been my age, so I took Alicja's birth certificate and went to live with my new "mother." Her family was starving, and she was unable to feed them, because she couldn't go out to work and leave the baby alone. The Jewish woman told my father, "If I can't save my own son, perhaps you can save your daughter."

There was no time for discussions, no time for other options, no time for other choices. My father decided that "becoming" Mrs. Tarasiuk's illegitimate daughter was the best and only choice.

And so I left the ghetto for good in October 1942. I became Alicja Szumlanska, the illegitimate daughter of Janina Szumlanska Tarasiukowa. Alicja's birth certificate now became mine.

Moving in and then living with Tarasiukowa as her illegitimate child, we planned our strategy very carefully. It was decided that the family would move into an apartment in a totally new section of Lwów, where no one knew us. The family consisted of me, Janina, two teen-aged boys, Jurek and Zdzich, four-year-old Cesia, and baby Andrew. Apartments were in very short supply due to bombings and lack of building materials. But as the ghetto was being liquidated, the empty buildings became available to the Christian population, while the wall surrounding the ghetto became tighter and tighter for those Jews still alive.

While Janina desperately looked for new living quarters, I stayed in her tiny apartment, hiding by day in a wooden wardrobe. She feared that if any of her friends, acquaintances, or neighbors should by some chance drop in to "visit," (not that people did much visiting in those days), they might find me not fitting in that scenario. Being savvy and street smart, Jurek and Zdzich knew that I was Jewish, and that I was supposed to be their illegitimate sister. Janina was sure that they would never be caught spilling the beans. Besides, they understood that my father was paying their mother to hide me, making it possible to keep from starving and put food on the table. Cesia, my little sister, had been told that I was her older sister who had been living with relatives in Krakow, but I had come back to help my family.

Our new apartment was located on the outskirts of the ghetto. It was a building that had perhaps twenty or more apartments and was filled with new Polish families. Janina quickly found a job in a meat factory, while I stayed home to take care of the baby, cook family meals, do the laundry and cleaning. I had no spare time, certainly no time for socializing with other girls, thus making sure that I got to know very few neighbors. I tried to have as little contact with other families as possible.

Having been an only child, I knew little of dealing with siblings and less about caring for a baby. I had to learn quickly and use common sense, since nothing was easy to obtain in those times; everything was in short supply. One made diapers out of a spare bed sheet, and when they were soiled, they were not thrown out but were washed, boiled, and hung on a line to dry. I had to use my imagination to take whatever food was available and concoct it into a mushy, palatable meal baby Andrew could swallow, something nourishing, or else he'd cry.

Young "Alice" had to learn fast, because my new mother, Janina, could not tolerate my mistakes. She really was a mean, greedy woman, demanding and impatient, though she needed me almost as much as I needed her. I had no choice but to obey her.[8]

In late 1943, a stranger arrived at our door. It was Kazimierz Tarasiuk, Janina's estranged husband, who had been released from a German prison, having been captured by the Nazis while serving in the Polish army. Janina had been separated from him before the war, because there was no divorce among the Catholics. Having returned to Poland, he wanted to see his children, and, frankly, he had no other place to stay. His children were three years older since he'd last seen them. Additionally, there were two strangers in Tarasiukowa's apartment: a Jewish girl pretending to be Janina's illegitimate child and baby Andrew, whose father was unknown to Mr. T.

It was agreed, that Mr. T would tolerate me, let me stay as part of "his" family, and not report me to the police. He turned out to be a very decent, honest man, a true "mensch," a much better human being than his wife. He also promised to adopt Andrew and give the baby his last name, providing that Janina would not see her lover again. She made the promise.

Although my existence with Tarasiukowa seemed quite secure, there were instances that might have become dangerous.

On one occasion, a nosy neighbor chatted with Janina in the corridor and remarked that I did not look at all like her. Such a comment was not an innocent remark. People were deeply suspicious then, and the neighbor may have suspected that I was a Jew living on false papers. Luckily, my "mother" had the presence of mind to reply to the neighbor that I

---

8   There were no washing machines back then, no hot water in the pipes, no clothes dryers. And what about those cute little Gerber jars with delicious peach, bananas, or applesauce or tasty green spinach, orange carrots that one feeds charming plump little babies today? Baby food in glass jars did not exist in those days.

resembled my father, and that Mr. T was not my father—a statement that put an end to the conversation.

On another occasion, another neighbor or possibly the same neighbor made the comment to Janina that she'd watched me doing the washing. "Alicja wrings the laundry like a Jew," she said, obviously insinuating that I was Jewish.

Had the neighbor reported us and had her assumption been proven correct, she might have received a bottle of liquor, some chocolates, a loaf of bread, or a used army jacket for her efforts and following Nazi orders.

After all, it would only have been a Jewish life for one of the wonderful prizes—and one fewer Jew to bother them, even if they didn't know their victim.

As Jews were eliminated constantly, ghetto borders got smaller and smaller. Poles moved into the dwellings, newly emptied of Jews. Thus after a few weeks, the Tarasiuk family, myself included, moved into an empty apartment in a different section of the city near the ghetto.

Janina started me on a crash course in learning Catholic prayers, hymns, and holy days. I had to be well versed in prayers like The Hail Mary and The Lord's Prayer, reciting the rosary, and many Polish saints, in case I were questioned or tricked by nosy people. I learned my lessons fast and well. I didn't know a tenth about my Jewish religion as I knew about Catholicism, but I knew that Jesus was a Jew, a fact that was never mentioned. One could wake me up in the middle of the night and I'd be able to answer any Catholic questions or recite any prayers.

Every so often, Tarasiukowa would send Jurek or Zdzich to the factory where my father worked to collect payment for my keeping. They were good kids, by and large, and quite trustworthy.

Cesia, though, was more of a problem. Sometimes she'd hiss at me, saying that I was not her sister. If someone overheard her, it would be fatal for all of us. She was a mean child, and I had trouble handling her. I had to share a bed with her, which she wet every night, only to claim that I was the one who'd done it.

I had to take care of everything—cooking, cleaning, washing laundry, and taking care of the baby. Because my housekeeping duties kept me very busy, I had no time to go out with other young girls, and that suited me just fine. Staying home was the safest place for me. And the neighbors believed that I had no time to go out or socialize.

Janina was not a nice person. She took the few pieces of my mother's clothing I was able to bring and fashioned an elegant outfit with a nutria collar for herself. She wore that outfit all through the war while my heart broke, seeing her wear it. She'd shout at me, scold me, curse me, and criticize me. She called me stupid and dumb. That kind of constant brainwashing was enough to make me despondent and more depressed. I sometimes wondered why I'd never been called stupid before I'd come to live with her. I lost confidence and became completely dependent on her. Even so, I was alone, friendless, with no one to talk to. I'd just lost my mother and had to behave like a normal, happy teenager, performing duties that were new to me. By trial and error, I had to find food that could be mashed and easy for the baby to eat, such as potatoes, carrots, and milk—if we were lucky to get it. Food was scarce then, and one had to use creativity. Soap was scant and of poor quality, so I had to use elbow grease to scrub laundry on a washboard with cold water, lugging heavy pails of water up three flights of steps. Every household chore was an undertaking, but I didn't mind hard work and I learned fast. Even so, I lived in constant fear that someone would come to our apartment, someone I'd known under different circumstances, who would recognize me, and I'd be arrested.

One day, Daddy sent instructions for me to come with one of my "brothers" to the factory. We met in a little room where no one could hear us; he told me that he had obtained false papers of a *Volksdeutscher* and that he'd rented a secret room on the "outside" where he would stay after the ghetto was liquidated. When he felt that the situation had calmed down, he planned to dress in lederhosen and a Tyrolean hat, go to the railroad station, buy a ticket, and board a train to Germany. Dressed that way with his Aryan looks and perfect German, he had a good chance of never being questioned and living in Germany until the war ended.

Then he showed me a little white pill that he kept in his belt buckle —
cyanide, the fastest acting poison. Daddy said that if he got caught, he
wouldn't let the Germans torture or kill him. He also told me he couldn't
write to me anymore, because it was too dangerous and getting mail would
create questions and suspicion. During the war years, people didn't write
letters and receiving mail from other countries created curiosity and suspicion. He told me to be a good, brave girl and that we were going to see
each other after the war. I hugged him and kissed him many times, and
then I left the factory.

When I first went to live with the Tarasiuk family, I received short
letters from my father. I always destroyed the letters after I read them. One
day, the letters and the money for Janina stopped coming; the news was
that the ghetto had been completely liquidated. There was no more ghetto
and no more Jews in Lwów.

My life with Tarasiukowa was not only difficult because of food
shortages and a scarcity of necessities but I was living with strangers, with
whom I had nothing in common. I missed my father and mother so terribly.

Our new apartment was located near the ghetto where Nazis were
constantly rounding up Jews. Often during the day, I'd hide behind a cur-
tained window, watching as Jews were driven in trucks to be shot or transported to concentration camps. I watched SS commandos going to and
from the ghetto. I hid from view and watched Jews being led to Piaski
or to be gassed. I never discussed with the family what I saw through the
window. I was living a constant lie. On some occasions, I saw groups of
Jews led out of the ghetto, carrying bags and suitcases, headed to the railroad station that would take them, I later learned, to Bełżec. At that time,
I thought that their carrying luggage gave them a glimmer of hope, and
that perhaps, just perhaps, they would be resettled somewhere. Neighbors
in our building talked about these activities like it was a normal occurrence. After every *akcja*, Poles would run to the empty apartments to plun-
der furniture, clothing, and valuables left behind by the Jewish families,
whom the Nazis rushed from their rooms as quickly as possible. Poles and
Ukrainians would sell their newly acquired loot on the black market, not in

the least concerned about people who'd had to abandon their possessions and march off to their deaths.

One day, Jurek or Zdzich brought back a comforter or *pierzyna* from an abandoned apartment. It was in great condition, large and light, full of goose down, but also full of lice. We had to throw it out because we had no way to disinfect bedding.

Once in a while I had to leave the apartment in order to show the neighbors that I was just like any other teenager and needed to be out. Usually, I made a big production of my outing, making certain that neighbors saw me leaving the building. I always took Andrew with me in my arms. If I saw a familiar face in the street, I'd hide my face behind the baby's. Often I went to church, the safest place to be, and after all, I was a good Catholic girl. I frequently suffered from nightmares. I grieved for my mother, crying quietly into the covers to hide my emotions. I did my best to behave like a normal teenager, as if I truly belonged to the family Tarasiuk.

Janina would often take me with her to church, telling me to stay in a side chapel, while she went to meet with her lover in another part of the church. Kazimierz Tarasiuk had stopped going to church long ago, so Janina knew he'd never catch them there. She also knew that I wouldn't tell him what had happened in the church; my life depended on my keeping mum.

My life did not change a great deal after Pan Tarasiuk's return. He tried to work around the house and he looked for jobs, but in the war-torn Lwów, businesses had ceased operating and everything was at a standstill. Somehow, the Tarasiuk family managed to survive, having saved some money my father had sent before he left the ghetto, as well as her earnings from the meat plant. She often was able to bring home animal blood, kidneys, brains, or a tongue—meats I'd not eaten before the war, but we were all hungry, and I prepared them well.

The Germans advertised that young strong Poles were needed for jobs in Germany; all German men and boys had been drafted into the army. Jurek decided to go to Germany to seek work. Once he left, we didn't hear from him.

Gerda's false identification photo as Alicja Szumlanska

Gerda's cousins Lila (left) and Irka Oberhard, Zygmunt Schwarzer,
and his girlfriend, Renia, in Przemysl

Gerda holding baby Andrew and Cesia

Zdzich Tarasiuk, Gerda's "brother"

Janina Tarasiukowa, Gerda's "mother" (after WWII)

END OF THE WAR

The newspapers were full of propaganda. News trickled in, but it was hard to know if it was true. We knew that the Nazis were losing the war, and that the Russians were moving westward, but we did not know whether to believe reports of concentration camps, gas chambers, and ovens. How could human beings commit such atrocities? Even by the spring of 1945, Germans were "relocating" Jewish remnants to camps, and young German soldiers continued fighting and dying at the front. Still, I held out hope that I'd soon reunite with my father and other relatives.

And then a day came when the Nazis were gone! The war was finally over. There was no excitement, no happiness in "our" family. The only way it affected me was in knowing the Nazis had been defeated and that I'd survived. Life had not changed; we continued living the way we'd been living under Nazi rule, only now we were again under the Soviet regime. The same terrible conditions remained: bed bugs, lice, loneliness, little to eat, and nothing to look forward to. I contacted the International Red Cross, leaving my address and inquiring about the whereabouts of my father and other relatives.

I looked through the window and saw two people walking down the street, both pale, their knees buckling under them. I realized they were Jews who must've been in hiding for a long time. Now that they were out, they could once again enjoy sunshine and learn how to use their legs, having spent months or years sitting in one position. Jews had been hiding in forests, cellars, sewers, holes, and bunkers. They depended on non-Jews who knew their hideouts and were willing to supply them with food and other necessities. Those who were hidden had to pay for food and other expenses and often when money had run out, the help ended. Many of those victims had to come out of hiding and most likely were caught and killed shortly afterward.

I thought that from that point on, there would be world peace, people would respect one other, life would return to normal, and there would be no more wars. How naive and foolish I was! Tarasiukowa wanted me to remain with her family. After all, I was both daughter and slave to her; she'd never find another servant like me. Having lived with Tarasiukowa for over three years, I was completely isolated from any other Jews. I felt I had to stay with Tarasiukowa until my family was found through the Red Cross.

I anxiously awaited news from my father. I hoped that a family member would try to contact me. After many weeks, I did receive a reply from the Red Cross that my cousin, Zygmunt Schwarzer, had miraculously survived Auschwitz and Bergen-Belsen. He was living in a displaced persons camp in Feldafing, Germany, ironically a former summer camp for Hitler Youth.

I didn't realize that immediately following the war, dozens of Jewish agencies had sprung up in every large European city, helping survivors reunite with family members who had been scattered throughout countries during the war. I'd been disconnected from any Jewish contact for a long time.

Apart from finding my family, the most important purpose in the nearest future was to go back to school to complete five lost years of my education. But it was too soon for such notions; for one thing, schools had not yet reopened. And certainly, no one in the Tarasiuk household mentioned or thought about education. The situation remained as it was; I was stuck.

Tarasiukowa had her own plan: to collect any and all of my parents' valuables, hidden in Przemyśl with Christian friends before our move to

Lwów. She was in a hurry to recoup payment for keeping me. She didn't acknowledge all the duties I'd performed for her family as reparation. Even so, I felt I owed her everything I could recover, since payments from my father had ceased. In fact, I was happy to give her all of these possessions. She had saved my life. For that I was very grateful.

Most of the valuables had been left with the headmistress of the *Gimnazjum* I'd attended. The headmistress had been my father's client, and my parents trusted her completely. In the summer of 1945 Kazimierz Tarasiuk and I traveled to Przemyśl to the home of the headmistress. I knew that the headmistress had hidden oriental rugs, a Singer sewing machine, my mother's fur coat, other clothing, paintings, fine china and objects that the Soviets and Nazis hadn't gotten their hands on.

The summer of 1945 was extremely hot. The roads were full of Soviet trucks and carts with horses, people going east and west, uncertain about where to move. Przemyśl was about 200 kilometers from Lwów. We didn't have luggage and walked with the crowds. My shoes pinched and the road was full of ruts and holes, dust and rocks. After a time, I took my shoes off and walked barefoot. Suddenly I noticed blood oozing from my foot; a stone must have cut the back of my left heel. The only thing I had to stop the bleeding was a handkerchief, so I tied it tightly around my foot. Amazingly, despite the filthy road and lack of dressing or antiseptic, my wound didn't get infected and healed after a few days without any treatment or dressings, forming a deep scar, a reminder of our crazy trip to Przemyśl.

We had no idea how long it would take us to get to Przemyśl, and my limp slowed us down. We tried to hitch a ride with Russian truck drivers, and after many attempts, we got lucky. A Russian soldier stopped his truck and told us to climb into the back; he was headed to Przemyśl. I was grateful to be able to finally sit and nurse my foot. When we got to Przemyśl, we thanked the Russian soldier and left him.

I took Pan Tarasiuk to the house where I used to live. There were no familiar faces and I didn't knock on any doors. I didn't even find out who occupied our old apartment. It was an odd sensation seeing the house so neglected and unkempt. The walls inside were cracked and in need of paint, the wooden doors were faded and peeling, the corridor floors were full of holes. Some of the windowpanes were broken or missing. Getting a new glass was out of the question. It made me sad, remembering how lovely and well kept the building had looked before the war. We walked around the city, not quite knowing where to go or whom to speak to.

At one point, we were standing in the midst of a crowded *Rynek*, marketplace, people milling about, trying to see if, by chance, they might encounter survivors, their own families, or people they knew before the war—any familiar face. As we were standing there, a young man came up to me and asked if I was Gerda Krebs.

"Yes!" I answered, though I didn't recognize him. I hadn't heard my true name spoken aloud for more than three years. Hearing it spoken aloud gave me a strange sensation—as if I'd returned from another life, another existence.

He continued, "I know what happened to your father. Do you want to know?"

I was shocked hearing this information, especially because this was Przemyśl not Lwów. How could a stranger know anything about my father who lived in a different city?

"Yes, of course," I replied.

He then told me that my father had rented a room on the "outside," in the Aryan section of Lwów and had hoped to use that "secret" room after the ghetto had been liquidated of Jews. Apparently, some men had begged my father to take them with him, to save their lives. As my father was leaving the ghetto for good and had always been a generous man, he had agreed. "Because your father did not look Jewish, he was the only one who dared to leave the room to search for food for all of them. While he was on the street, a Pole or Ukrainian must have recognized him and pointed a finger at him."

Without waiting for me to speak or react to his startling revelations, the young man turned in the other direction and walked off. I didn't know his name; didn't know how he knew my father or how he'd recognized me. It was a mystery. But I was devastated by his account, and I feared he'd spoken the truth. I knew then that I'd never see my father again nor learn who the young man was and how he knew all these facts.

That afternoon, I went to see a doctor in town. His name was familiar to me from years before. He had opened an office in the *Rynek*. He asked me in. We went through his waiting room, which contained several odd chairs only. It was bare otherwise. Next we entered into the examining room that contained an ancient X-ray machine, an examining table, and a couple of chairs. We spoke for a while, telling each other how we'd survived, and though we were total strangers, I felt a strong connection with him. A Catholic woman from Przemyśl had hidden him, he said, and at war's end, he'd married her. There were many cases like his, where a hidden Jew married his or her "savior," usually a young Polish man or woman who'd forfeited their own safety. In fact, the doctor had known my parents; unfortunately, he had no information for me about them or about others in town I'd known.

Another thing I learned from the doctor was that my ex-headmistress no longer lived in Przemyśl. She and her husband had moved to northwestern Poland. I obtained their new address—I don't remember how or from whom.

Pan Tarasiuk and I returned to Lwów with empty hands. Lwów had been a lively, cosmopolitan city before the war, one of the largest in Poland, but it had turned into a derelict ruin, its buildings heavily bombed or obliterated during bombing. The roads were full of holes, there was no electricity and no services whatsoever. People had to cope the best they could.

Janina wanted me to collect the hidden items from the director of school. She gave me money for a railroad ticket to travel to northwestern Poland. I traveled all night, arriving in town the next morning. It didn't take me long to find the house with the name of the headmistress. I rang the bell full of anticipation to see the woman I'd admired and respected. She opened the door slightly, recognizing me at once. She was very surprised to see me, perhaps thinking I'd been murdered along with so many other Jews by Nazis or their collaborators. She didn't ask me in. She didn't even offer me a glass of water. She barely kept the door ajar. She told me that before she moved to her new place, she'd mailed the trunk with my family's belongings to people in the Carpathian Mountains for safekeeping. She wrote an address on a piece of paper, and closed the door.

I stood in front of the closed door. I didn't have the presence of mind to invite myself inside. I walked away, realizing that the reason she kept me outside was that in all likelihood our carpets were on her floor, our sewing machine was in her room, our paintings were hanging on her walls. She didn't want me to see anything. I knew better than to go back and argue with her; I couldn't prove that she was lying. The country was in total chaos, and there was no law to protect the innocent. One had to depend on human decency and honesty, and there was precious little of that.

Janina was relentless. She sent me to the mountains to find the people who had supposedly received the trunk, but that trip, too, proved fruitless. No one seemed to know anything about it. I wrote many letters to the headmistress, who eventually replied, as if I were bothering her, that my parents' valuables had apparently been lost on the train en route to the Carpathian Mountains. It seemed untrue, and all because I was trying to recover what was rightfully mine.

Pan Tarasiuk had begun making candles in the apartment, using paraffin and string. He fashioned a wheel with nails and on each nail he'd hang a long string, pouring hot paraffin while turning the wheel. Eventually, each of the strings accumulated enough paraffin to become a candle. Each day I'd take a large basket of candles to sell in the market; in this way, the Tarasiuks had new means to feed the family. But there were many other candle makers who were dishonest. They wouldn't put full strings into the candles but a tiny tip of a string at the very end to make them look like a whole candle. People would buy them, bring them home, and light them, but the candles would soon sputter and die.

The market was the place where all the business was transacted. Wheelers and dealers sold everything from used dishes, shoes, and clothing to food from the countryside, such as fruit and vegetables, sometimes even meat and a few skinny chickens or kielbasa. Sugar was in short supply, so people had resorted to using saccharine. Saccharine was sold in small amounts, a tablespoon at a time, wrapped in tissue paper, then folded into a stronger paper, in order to prevent spillage. A packet of saccharine could sweeten a large pot of coffee or tea, or a large amount of food. Saccharine grains looked like sugar, but were far sweeter.

Dishonest merchants would substitute a tablespoon of regular sugar for saccharine, barely enough to sweeten a cup of tea, let alone a large pot. Peasants skimmed cream from milk, resulting in a thin, bluish liquid. They added a bit of carrot juice to make it appear richer, as if it contained cream. Because milk was not pasteurized, it had to be boiled at home before it was used. Unfortunately, the milk containing the added carrot juice would curdle as soon it came to a boil and the whole amount had to be discarded. Food was in short supply and very expensive; one could only hope that what they bought would be edible and not spoiled. Pretty soon, customers learned who the trustworthy salesmen were. Since the candles Pan Tarasiuk made were well made, I developed regular customers. I was proud to be an honest seller. I was always hungry while selling the candles and the market was full of fresh food being sold by the peasants. The food was so tempting, but Janina knew exactly how many candles I brought to market and how much money they would fetch. And woe to me if my money wasn't the correct amount!

While selling my candles I walked around the carts displaying ripe fruits, fresh tempting vegetables, scrumptious cheeses, and baked goods. I often sampled items, and pretended I didn't like them so that I wouldn't have to buy them. I'd take a cherry or a strawberry, take a small bite, shake my head as if I didn't like it, and move on to the next cart. I could have eaten all the sweet fruits with gusto, but I didn't dare to spend even a few kopecks on a piece of bread or an apple. I was that afraid of Janina.

In the fall of 1945, the Russian government gave Polish citizens an option to either stay in Lwów and become Russian citizens or to go west beyond the new border in order to keep their Polish citizenship. The Tarasiuks decided to leave Lwów, and I went with them. It was a golden Polish autumn. We traveled in a cattle train, but one that had the gates open, unlike trains that took Jews to the camps. I didn't realize that Jews had gone to concentration camps in the exact same cars that we were on; the major difference was that we were free to get on or off the train at any time.

After several days we reached the city of Poznań in northwestern Poland. Janina's brother had moved from Lwów to Poznań months before and had secured a one-room apartment for us in the same bombed-out building where he lived. There were six of us altogether: Pan and Pani Tarasiuk, Zdzich, Cesia, baby Andrew, and me.

We occupied a ten-by-eighteen-foot room with one window, covered in cardboard, the glass having been broken. In those post-war years, one could not get window glass at any price. Living in such tight quarters was hell. The single room served as our bedroom, kitchen, washroom, and living room. The walls were filled with bedbugs that came out to feed on our blood every night. All we could do was to squash the blood-sucking critters during the night, though we were half asleep. We had body lice that laid eggs in the seams of our clothing and feasted on our blood by day and night. It was impossible to get rid of them unless one could bathe and burn the lice-infested clothing. We had no way of improving the situation.

We had one gas burner for cooking and heating water. Toilets were located outside in the corridor. I rarely left the room since it was very cold and I had only a single pair of torn shoes and no warm clothing. I had no money and no place to go. Besides, I was too busy taking care of Andrew, cooking, washing, and cleaning.

All through the war, I'd lived and carried on just to survive, hoping to see my father and other relatives again one day. And when the war was over, that hope was gone. Though my life was no longer threatened, it remained hopeless, grim, and depressing with no future. The whole country was in total disorder; there was no law except for those who had guns or muscles. Schools did not function, shops were empty, and nothing was normal. No culture, no music, no life of any sort. Secretly, I wondered if making it through the war had really been an advantage. I was so unhappy and lonely and miserable. I had no future staying with the Tarasiuk family. My despondence deepened. I considered suicide.

In November 1945, I received a letter from a friend of my parents, who'd found me through the Red Cross. Tarasiukowa opened the envelope and read the letter before she handed it to me. No privacy whatsoever. She had to know what the letter was about before I read it. Mrs. Rysia Masłowska, whose teenaged daughter had been murdered by the Nazis, lived in Katowice. She survived the war by living on false papers. She invited me to come live with her. She offered to care for me, promising to send me to the university, even offering to adopt me. But by then I was too old to be adopted and I had had one beloved mother and no one could ever replace Mamusia.

Mrs. Masłowska's invitation seemed like a gift from heaven. She enclosed money in the envelope for a train ticket, but greedy Janina removed the 250 zloty from the envelope, waving it before my eyes. "May I borrow it?" she asked, and she and I both knew it wasn't a question. "Yes," I answered weakly. She further told me that she couldn't possibly allow me to leave until she found a replacement for me and once again I agreed to wait. Janina wielded great power over the whole family and, frankly, we were all afraid of her.

I wanted to reply to Mrs. Masłowska to thank her for her kind invitation, but I didn't even have enough money for stamps! Mr. Tarasiuk secretly gave me money for postage so that I could reply to her and correspond with my family in England whom I'd also found through the Red Cross. I had to question whether I was in my right mind to work for the Tarasiuks without pay, living in a dismal, dirty room. Janina didn't fool me, but I acted as if I believed her promise to find my replacement, knowing full well she'd never find anyone willing to work as I did for no pay. Even so, I waited and hoped. Weeks went by, and nothing changed.

Every couple of weeks, I'd weakly ask if she'd found anyone, but she emphatically answered "Not yet!" I had no one to ask for advice or help. Depressed though I was, I talked to myself. *"Daddy saved me from the Holocaust, the war is over, and I'm free… so how can I still be afraid and under the clutches of Janina Tarasiukowa? I have to collect my courage to tell her I need the money that she took from me to buy a train ticket because I'm leaving."*

Finally, a day arrived when I overcame my fear and decided to leave that evening. I packed my belongings into a small box. I had so little to carry—no change of clothing, no mementos, photographs, or personal articles, except for one precious little knit scarf that belonged to my mother. It was the only memento that Tarasiukowa let me keep. Memories of my parents I kept deep down in my heart. During the war, it had been too dangerous for me to have any connection of any sort with my family, since I led a life of lies and false papers, a false name, a false birth certificate, and a false religion.

That day in January of 1946, when Janina came home from work, and with my heart racing, I announced, "I'm leaving today, and I need 250 zloty for the ticket." The woman became incensed, screaming how ungrateful I was. "Is this how you repay me for saving your life?" I squirmed. I couldn't speak, I wondered if I should renege on my decision and stay. After her fury and outrage, I kept quiet while she went upstairs to her brother's apartment to borrow the money for my ticket. I had doubts if I was doing the right thing. Had I been unfair to her? Should I have waited longer for a better time? But then her husband approached me on the sly, whispering, "If you don't leave today, Alka, you'll never escape this miserable life." Pan Tarasiuk gave me the encouragement and confidence I dearly needed. I was so innocent in those days; he could have exploited me or taken advantage of me if he'd wanted, but he never did. He was an honorable man.

When Janina returned with the money, I took it and hurriedly and left. Outside, the streets were dark, and a bitter wind blew. In snow and darkness, I walked to the railroad station. The station was mayhem. There was no order, no proper police. The trains ran irregularly, arriving early, late, or not at all. I purchased a ticket to Katowice and somehow found the platform where the train was scheduled to depart. I boarded the train and found each wagon packed to capacity. Corridors were overcrowded, and there was no space to stand. I searched one compartment after another, from the first to the last wagon. Fortunately, I found a seat in a cabin sometimes used by a conductor. It was cold and cramped, a few steps above the regular car and reeked of urine, but it would get me out of the city. My satisfaction lasted fewer than five minutes, because suddenly a Russian soldier appeared with a girl in tow and ordered me out. He had power and I did not. I descended the steps, fearful and anxious, trying again to get inside the stuffed train. Some people climbed on the roof, having nowhere else to go. I stood on steps outside of one wagon, holding onto the door as the engine started chugging and the train slowly began to move. I wasn't entirely sure I was on the right train, but I gripped the freezing door handle as it picked up speed. I was leaving Poznań! As the train sped along, wind whipped through my thin jacket, and my hair blew every which way. I was determined to hold on for dear life, to get away. Riding on the outside of the speeding rail car, I kept telling myself, *"Hold on tight to the frozen handle no matter what. Your future depends on leaving Poznań now and getting to Katowice."* After a long while—maybe one hour or maybe just thirty minutes—the train stopped at a station, and a few people got off. And I was able to go inside the train and find a seat on a bench. I was grateful for the warmth and a place to sit.

By morning, the train arrived in Katowice. It was Sunday, church bells were ringing for early Mass, and virgin snow covered the streets. It was quiet and peaceful with almost empty streets in the early morning hour.

For a moment, I considered stopping at the church for a quick prayer before meeting Mrs Masłowska, but I gave up that idea the next moment. I wasn't living with Janina anymore and didn't have to abide by her rules.

Holding the envelope with Mrs. Masłowksa's address, I asked a few pedestrians where I'd find her street. The handwriting on the envelope wasn't very clear, and the first house I tried was wrong. I went to another address, but it too was wrong. I became very nervous, wondering what I'd do or where I'd go if I couldn't locate Mrs. Masłowska. One thing I was sure of: I'd never under any circumstances go back to Poznań. Gathering my courage, I approached another stranger for help, and he pointed me to another street. The third building was solid, elegant, and well kept. I climbed three flights of stairs and rang the bell, my heart pounding. I fervently hoped it was the right house, that my friend would recognize me, and that she'd still be willing to put a roof over my head. I held my breath. The door swung open, and a tall, grey-haired woman took one look at me and started crying.

"Gerdusia," she said, "my poor child, come in." I looked like a ragamuffin. My hair was uncombed, my shoes torn, and my paper skirt and jacket were in shreds. Under my arm was my small paper package with all my belongings. She took me gently into in her arms and held me for a long while.

"Would you like to take a bath?" she asked

I hadn't had a bath in three years. "A bath?" was all I could think to answer. I couldn't believe my good luck. I was overjoyed, but my delight soon turned to worry. I had to tell her about the lice in my hair and clothes. I felt an overwhelming shame over my shabby appearance. I shouldn't have worried. Mrs. Masłowska surmised my situation and gave me some of her own clothing to wear, which she left in the bathroom, and I never laid eyes on my old lice-infested clothing again. It was a miracle; within days, both head and body lice were gone, and I wore clean underwear and clothes.

The next day, Mrs. Masłowska took me to a United Nations Relief Association (UNRA) office. This huge warehouse contained clothing sent from England and the United States for people like me. I received a good pair of shoes, a used skirt, and two blouses, pink and white, all items in perfect condition. Now I had a choice of blouses, an unimagined luxury. Imagine my feeling to suddenly become an owner of two blouses. Gosh! Which should I wear first, the pink or the white blouse? What a difficult decision! Having clean clothing and a clean bed to sleep in was a wonderful feeling, but to have a friend who cared for me and talked to me was even better.

Those first few days of freedom and the kindness of Mrs. Masłowska were remarkable. My friend was an emancipated woman, who even before the war, believed that women had rights and could think for themselves, that they could make their own choices and decisions. Soon after the war, she immersed herself in collecting data, taking photographs, interviewing Holocaust survivors and Poles who had hidden Jews. Each day, she'd travel to different neighborhoods of southwestern Poland.[9] She'd meet various people at Jewish Agencies, collecting information about how they'd been able to survive, if they'd been helped and by whom, whether they'd been deported to labor or concentration camps, and how they'd managed to stay alive. She typed all the information on her old typewriter, planning one day to write a book about their experiences.

One day, I walked into her living room and to my great surprise and joy, there was my uncle Henryk Leibel, sitting in a chair and smiling. The last news I'd had of him was a postcard sent from the Ural Mountains in 1941. Evidently, he had known Mrs. Masłowska and in the postwar chaos, he'd found her again and they had become friends. Now, to his delight, I was another surviving relative. I told him my family's story and asked questions about his own war experiences. We couldn't stop talking. His parents had died on the long train ride to Russia, but he had ended up working in Ural Mountains despite brutal conditions and had miraculously survived.

He told me that after he'd come back from Russia, he stopped in Przemyśl. Because he was a lawyer once, he'd taken the initiative, hoping

---

9 Katowice is not far from Oświęcim, the site of the concentration camp, Auschwitz.

that I'd somehow survived, of going to City Hall to register me as owner of Mother's building on Piłsudskiego Street, as I was my parents' only heir. Although I had no rights to any real estate ownership under the current Communist government, Uncle Leibel's quick thinking enabled me to eventually gain ownership of mother's building sometime in early 2000.[10]

One evening, Mrs. Masłowska said she'd heard about a Rabbi Solomon Schonfeld from London, currently staying in Warsaw, who was gathering a group of war orphans to travel to England. She knew I had relatives in Leeds, namely, my father's sister Eveline Krebs Mantel. With tremendous tact, she asked if I might prefer to join my relatives in England or stay with her—that she'd be happy to continue caring for me. She added that she'd pay for my education and that I could choose any school I wanted. It took me two seconds to make a decision. Grateful as I was for her friendship and generosity and for getting me out of an untenable situation with the Tarasiuks, I wanted to leave Poland, its oppressive regime, and the horrifying memories of the past five years. She further recommended that before I left, I should first try to regain possession of my mother's building—*my* building now.

I told her without hesitation, "To hell with that building! More than anything I want to get out of Poland. Our family lost so much more than a building. Living in a free world is more important than any structure."

Up until that moment of my declaration, leaving Poland seemed a totally impossible dream, as the Communists forbade emigration. Still, though I couldn't imagine what it would be like to live in a free, faraway country such as Great Britain, I knew any country would be better than Poland. Leaving Poland and living in England was as unlikely as planning a trip to the moon.

Once again, Mrs. Masłowska gave me money for a railroad ticket, and that evening I took the night train to Warsaw.

---

10   Mrs. Masłowska had hoped to marry my uncle for companionship in her late years, but the marriage never happened. Uncle Henryk left Poland for Palestine and Mrs. Masłowska emigrated to Israel several years later.

The next morning as I left the train station in Warsaw, I saw a city totally destroyed. Before the war, Warsaw had often been called little Paris, but now it was in ruins. As far as the eye could see, there was nothing but rubble and destruction. Skeletons of buildings hinted at once magnificent edifices. There were no streets and no street names. Roads were torn up, and one had to climb over rocks and stones, watching for deep holes, most of them filled with rainwater or melting snow.

It was six o' clock in the morning, and I was hungry. To my surprise, I saw a woman with a small cart, selling sausages and black bread. I bought a piece of sausage and a chunk of bread and ate them while sitting on a rock. I worried that it might be too early to try to meet Rabbi Schonfeld. He was staying at the Hotel Polonia, the only building still standing in the center of Warsaw and located very close to the railroad station.

I entered the hotel, waiting in the lobby until a decent hour. At around 8:00 a.m., I took the elevator to the third floor. The door opened automatically and I found myself in a long noisy corridor with many children and a few adults running to and fro. A man approached me, asking in Yiddish why I was there. As I didn't speak Yiddish, I answered in Polish.

"I'm wondering if I'm in the right place? I'm looking for Rabbi Schonfeld. I want to go to England."

It was unreasonable, expecting to travel right away to England, a foreign country. But I needed to get away from the place that had brought such pain, sadness, fear, poverty, and destruction. I desperately wanted to find freedom, to get an education, to locate relatives, maybe even find happiness once more. I knew it was chutzpah and bravado that made me speak in such a way to a stranger.

The man responded in Polish, asking if I had relatives in England and why I wanted to go there.

"I lost my whole family in Poland. My father's sister lives in Leeds and I hope to live with her. She sent me a letter, inviting me to stay with her." I held out the letter, and he read it.

Then I saw HIM, a tall handsome man with bright blue eyes and a long black beard, wearing a British Officer's uniform with many medals on his chest: Rabbi Solomon Schonfeld. He approached us, and the Polish man showed him the letter from my aunt. The rabbi read it and nodded, saying that yes, I could go to England, and that I would be a part of his transport of war orphans.

The man interpreted for the rabbi. He said that we'd be leaving from Gdynia in March and that I'd be notified where to report. I couldn't comprehend the words he uttered, as it had happened so quickly. I was stunned. Then the elevator door opened, and a man emerged holding a small child by the hand. He began to beg both the man and the rabbi to take his boy to England.

"Please!" he said. "I'll get to England somehow, but please, please take my child on the transport!" Not unkindly, the man informed him that the list was closed and he couldn't take more children. He pointed to me, saying, "This girl is last on our list."

My good fortune didn't escape me. Had I waited another fifteen minutes before going to see the rabbi, the little boy would have been the last on the list, and I would've been left behind in Poland.

I returned to Katowice and told my benefactress my good luck, that I'd been accepted for transport to England in six weeks. She said she was sorry to see me go but she felt that I'd be much better off going to England than staying with her. While in Katowice, Mrs. Masłowska introduced me to Anita S. and her mother, both survivors from Lwów. Anita and I became good friends.[11]

Six weeks passed in a flash, and I flew from Warsaw to Gdynia, a port on the Baltic. It was my first airplane flight, and we were told that we should have a lemon and a paper bag, because the plane wasn't pressurized and we could suffer airsickness. The whole plane was filled with war orphans leaving Poland. I was too excited to be sick, but I sucked on the lemon anyway, the first I'd seen in six years.

---

11   Our friendship continued until Anita passed away two years ago.

We boarded a Swedish ship. In the middle of the night, we set sail, traveling the Baltic and the North Sea to England. We were all very enthusiastic and happy to leave Poland with its memories of the horrors and murders of the Shoah. I shared the cabin with three other girls, but once the ship left the port, I became seasick and spent most of the trip vomiting and in bed. We never asked each other where we'd come from or how we'd survived, nor did we exchange names. Perhaps, if I hadn't been so ill, I might have made new friends and kept in contact with them, but the choppy seas didn't relent for six days. We left Gdynia in the middle of the night, and in the morning, I woke up feeling nauseated, a dim light filtering through the porthole. Outside, the sea danced up and down, waves beating against the ship, my stomach matching its twists and turns. Needless to say, I couldn't rouse myself when we were called for breakfast and stayed in bed. Some passengers fared much better, unaffected by roiling seas.

One girl came to my cabin, excitedly announcing that sardines would be served at lunch, a food we hadn't seen since war broke out. But the very thought of sardines made me even queasier.

I remember Rabbi Schonfeld teaching us some English words and songs:

> *Oh, it ain't gonna rain no more, no more*
> *It ain't gonna rain no more*
> *How in the heck will I wash my neck*
> *if it ain't gonna rain no more?*

The other song that I learned and remembered was the popular tune, "You Are My Sunshine." This song has many meanings for me, and each time I hear it, I see the ship's deck with the wonderful rabbi, teaching us the words.

> *You are my sunshine, my only sunshine*
> *You make me happy when skies are gray*
> *You'll never know dear, how much I love you*
> *Please don't take my sunshine away.*

What did the words mean to lonely kids going into the unknown? They made me think about my mother, whom I had lost at age fourteen, and I tried to imagine that she was still near me and would always watch over me.

We arrived in Southampton on March 1, 1946. After going through many formalities, we finally disembarked and were able to put our feet on terra firma. Some children were taken to a shelter or home in London, where they remained for a long time. I had no idea where I would end up that day. Most of the orphans would stay in a hostel provided by a Jewish agency, because they had no relatives to stay with and no other destination. Some planned to go to Palestine, others had relatives as I did, but the rabbi and the English committee took care of all the arrangements.

I spotted a slim young man who reminded me of Uncle Moric Gottlieb from Przemyśl. When he saw me, he ran over and started hugging me. It was, in fact, Ludwik Gottlieb, my third cousin once removed on my father's side. I'd only met him once in Przemyśl when I was little, but even then he bore a strong resemblance to his father. Everyone called him Ludek (in Poland, nearly every name was made into a diminutive). When he finally let go of me, he looked me up and down.

"My goodness, how you have grown," he marveled. Somehow he thought I had remained the same age, six or seven.

The formalities and the trip to London took several hours. I'd packed a small trunk of clothes that I'd accumulated in Katowice. I sat on a bus in awe of others and how polite they were — schoolgirls in hats and uniforms, laughing and babbling in a language I didn't understand. The single word I understood was "yes." In those first days in London, English sounded incomprehensible to my ears. How would I ever learn and understand those impossible sounds? The city itself was overwhelming, its crowds of people, the way they were dressed, red double-decker buses and streetcars, stores that looked grand, although England had just begun to recover from bombings during the war. Comparing it to Poland, it was luxurious.

Nothing else mattered. I was in London! What a glorious feeling, so indescribable, so amazing, so English! Three months before, I'd been destitute, depressed and desperate, with no future or hope, no way of improving my lot. And now I was in London without cares or fear. I didn't speak English and most British people didn't speak Polish, so we had no way of communicating. I never thought of this problem before I left Poland, but having my cousin speak Polish solved the problem upon arrival.

Cousin Ludek took me by several buses to the center of London. He brought me to his tiny flat where his wife, Joan, and baby son, Stephen, were both sick in bed. Joan spoke only English. The Gottliebs' flat was tiny, just one room, so Ludek wanted to treat me by giving me a memorable welcome to London and a deluxe one for a young orphan from Poland. Later I found out that booking a room for me at the hotel was quite a financial sacrifice, because the Gottliebs had to count their pennies. Joan was a nurse but was not working then, having just given birth. And the BBC where Ludek worked didn't pay much. Ludek and I waved to Joan and left for the hotel.

Ludek advised me that since I spoke no English, when I went to the dining room the next morning, I should say "Yes, please," to all the questions that the waitress would ask. He told me that breakfast came with the hotel room and I could have anything that was offered. He told me he'd pick me up after breakfast before going to BBC.

Having a hotel room all to myself seemed grand. The bed was made up in a way I'd never seen before. The blanket and the counterpane were tucked tightly under the mattress. Not wanting to disturb the bed, I found it difficult sliding in between the sheets. The sheets were typically cold, almost damp, since the English weather was very damp. Eventually I slipped between the tight sheets and within minutes I was asleep.

The next morning, I dressed and feeling rather hungry, I took a lift downstairs to the dining room. I was seated at a table by the window with a white tablecloth and napkin and several pieces of cutlery. A friendly waitress asked a question and I said very proudly, "Yes, please." She brought me a pot of tea, a pitcher of milk, and a toast in a toast rack. I'd never seen a toast rack before. Then she asked me other questions and porridge appeared with cream and brown sugar on the side. I'd never eaten porridge, but it tasted delicious in my empty stomach. Next came a plate with two fried eggs, bacon, and bangers or English sausage—a delicious new taste— as well as a triangle of fried bread with baked beans. Evidently, I'd ordered everything on the menu, except for smoked Scottish trout. I had never eaten such a huge and delicious breakfast nor had I ever eaten so much at one meal. Reality began to sink in. I was in the fabulous city of London and had eaten an English breakfast in a hotel! It was a new world with strange people whom I couldn't understand, nor could they understand me. What a wonderful experience! I then waited for Ludek, but the wait seemed rather long, so I decided to go to his flat and surprise him.

When he opened the door, he was shocked.

"Why didn't you wait for me, Gerda? I told you I'd pick you up at the hotel."

"When you didn't come, I thought I'd come to your flat," I answered.

"But my dear child, you don't speak any English, what if you'd gotten lost?"

"But I didn't," I replied, proud of myself.

Ludek went to work, and I stayed home with Joan and the baby. Joan tried out her few Polish words, trying to teach me basic English vocabulary.

After a while, she and the baby fell asleep, as they were still under the weather. I decided to cook something for that night's dinner. I found enough food in the tiny little fridge to actually make a meal. I found some potatoes, enough flour and an egg for the dumplings and made *paluszki*, gnocchi in the form of a finger. I found bacon rinds with fat remaining, which Joan was going to throw out. Instead, I rendered the fat and fried onions in it. I also made peas and carrots with butter and brown sugar. When Ludek returned that evening from the BBC, I served them dinner. My cooking brought back memories for Ludek. He remarked how much my dishes tasted like his own mother's. He said it was the first time since leaving Poland that he'd eaten these dishes.

The next morning, I bade goodbye to Joan and baby Stephen. Ludek put me on a train going north to Leeds. Aunt Eveline was waiting for me at the station. She was a small, plump lady with white hair, rosy cheeks, and a sweet smile. I'd met my father's sister once before the war. It felt so good to live with a member of my family and to be able to converse with her. Of course, anything would be better than living in post-war Poland, and I expected that my future would be very different than it had been with Tarasiukowa in Poznań. I looked forward to meeting her husband, Uncle Molek, who used to stop in Przemyśl on business trips to Russia. In my haste to leave Poland, I hadn't given much thought to how I'd support myself or whether I'd be happy living with relatives. I hadn't made firm plans about schooling or a future profession. But I was positive in my outlook and determined to do my very best. First of all, I had to learn the language to be able to function in a new country, which so far had accepted me without any restrictions.

On the bus, Aunt Eva and I spoke Polish. She brought me to her home at 19 Ashgrove, where she lived with her husband and two sons, Walter and Fred. I was given my own room, an extravagance, and assigned a day of the week on which I might bathe, as heating was rationed; England was still suffering from shortages. If you missed your one designated day, you had to wait till the next week for that opportunity to bathe again. Certain foods were also rationed: sugar, butter, eggs, and meat. One had to have a coupon for clothing and shoes. But by comparison to the privations in Poland, everything seemed plentiful and lavish. Walter, my older cousin, counseled me to listen to the radio in order to get familiar with English. Try as I might, the only words I could make out in the jumble were "yes" and "no" and "please." My cousins spoke only German and English, so with my smattering of German, we could have a minimal conversation.

One day, a few days after my arrival, I ventured to do some shopping for my aunt. I went to the greengrocer, having memorized the words I'd need to ask for things at the store. I repeated the words all the way to the store: "I want to buy thick rhubarb. Please give me eight sticks." When I got to the shop, the greengrocer asked, "What do you want, loov (love)?" This form of endearment took me aback. *How dare he call me "loov" when we'd never met? Was he being fresh?* I couldn't answer him since my English vocabulary was limited. I just said, "I want sick rhubarb." In Yorkshire, calling someone love was common, similar to using "Miss" or "Mrs." I decided to ignore the way he addressed me and repeated the words I'd memorized. This made the greengrocer chuckle. "Sick rhubarb? Sick?" He held his head as if he had a headache. "You don't want sick rhubarb, loov, what you want is *thick* rhubarb." He repeated the word a few times more: *thick*. Politely I smiled, as he chose the rhubarb, but I couldn't understand why he was repeating the same words I'd used, over and over. I took coins from my purse, paid for the rhubarb, and he gave me change. Later, I related what had happened at the grocers to my aunt, and she laughed, explaining my mispronunciation.

You see, there is no "th" sound in the Polish language, so I had to learn that pronunciation and practice that sound. The pronunciation changed the meaning of the word. I wasn't alone; many foreigners have had the greatest trouble pronouncing "th" words and therefore speak English with a thick accent.

Both Walter and Fred, born in Vienna and raised in Munich, spoke fluent English and German. My German was minimal at best, so I couldn't converse with them. I understood the language better than I could speak. It was frustrating, not knowing how my life would turn out, but my main focus would be learning the new, baffling language and catching up with my neglected education.

My aunt thought that if I were to live with an English-speaking family, I might be able to learn English more quickly. She'd heard about Professor Vincent Benn, who taught French at Leeds University. His wife, Mildred, taught French in high school and English to foreign students during the summer. It was decided that I would go to live with the Benns that summer. They lived in Otley, a charming little township near Yorkshire Moors and Dales, a scant half hour from Leeds by bus.

One June day I packed my belongings into a suitcase and boarded a bus to Otley. Though I hadn't met the Benns, I was full of expectations and optimistic about learning English. It would certainly be another new experience for me. I got off the bus and walked via the directions I'd been given. Otley was a town with typical streets, shops, and flowers growing in front of stores and at street corners. I came upon a typical looking English home with a large rounded window of the master bedroom that faced a charming rose garden. Suitcase in hand, I rang the bell. A little blue-eyed blonde girl, Julia, opened the door and I immediately introduced myself as Gerda. She looked up at me with serious eyes. "Gerda," Julia said in her lovely British accent, "Do you know how to spell the word 'beautiful'?" In fact, I did know, and I spelled it for her slowly and carefully.

"Oh, Gerda" she said, "you're so clever!"

During the war I'd frequently been told how stupid I was, how badly I had done everything, and all of a sudden, I was told a moment after our meeting that I was clever, there on a strange threshold in England, simply said by a lovely little girl. What a promising introduction to the Benn family! I then met Mildred Benn, a tall, slender woman with a kind smile and friendly demeanor. Dr. Vincent Benn appeared, smiling and welcoming. Finally, I met Nicholas, an eight-year-old boy, who was quite serious but had the same smile as his father. They showed me "my" room along with the rest of the lived-in and cozy house, with its many books and articles piled everywhere.

They told me that from then on I was to speak only English, no matter how badly I mispronounced words or messed up grammar. When I made a mistake, I was told to try to correct it myself; the Benn children never laughed at my many mistakes and botched pronunciations. They informed me why a certain expression was wrong, or when I used the wrong grammar, so that I wouldn't repeat the same mistake. Since it was summer, there was no school for the children, so they spent all days with us. Each day after breakfast, I helped with the dishes, and then the four of us would go to a farm to buy fresh vegetables and greens, and strawberries for teatime. Everything was new to me, pleasant and enjoyable and so normal. The Benns didn't own a car; they never did. They either walked or took a bus, but bus transportation was very good. As we walked on the moors, Mildred named all the flowers and bushes we came upon during our climb. She had a vast knowledge of flora and enjoyed sharing it. We all loved being in the outdoors and absorbed Mildred's information. The children were never bored during our walks; they skipped, picked flowers, and asked their mother the names of plants, or remarked about everything they did or saw.

Our life was without stress and happy. While Vincent went to the University by bus each day, we tidied up the house. All four of us did household chores and spent afternoons in the garden, planting and weeding or walking the moors with its greenery and heather, its wildlife.

Teatime, an old English tradition, was an important meal of the day, during which the whole family gathered and discussed any subject that was interesting or new. The children participated in the conversation, telling stories or asking questions; they never interrupted when the adults spoke and always asked politely if they could be excused from the table, once they'd finished eating. Their good manners and politeness made a deep impression on me.

Mildred spent time teaching me the fundamentals of English, making it painless and easy to absorb. As the days passed, my speaking and understanding of English improved without my noticing it. I soon became comfortable in conversing with everyone, and most people congratulated me on how well I used the language.

In truth, my English wasn't as wonderful as all that. Most English people who spoke only their native language said they would never have made as much progress learning Polish as I had in English in such a short time. Nicholas liked to give me dictations on spelling. He'd quiz me on spelling and grammar. One day he dictated the word "weather" and while I understood there were two meanings and spellings for that word, I didn't know which one he meant. When I asked Nicholas which of the two words he wanted me to spell, he shyly replied, "You know, Gerda, I don't know myself." He was a lovely boy.

The summer months sped by, and when the fall arrived, I felt much better prepared to deal with my future. I said goodbye to the Benns and returned to Leeds. I wanted to get a job in a department store. We did not have large department stores in Poland and I thought that kind of work would be interesting and offer lots of experience and opportunities. After a couple of inquiries, I found out that such large stores would not hire foreigners who spoke with an accent. I almost got a job in a Jewish bakery in the Jewish section of Leeds, but the owner of the bakery often spoke Yiddish, and his wife expected me to help with the household. This job didn't sound like what I was looking for, and there was certainly no opportunity to improve my English.

In the postwar days, a foreigner in England could only get one of three jobs: nursing, domestic, and land army. Land army meant working on the farm or the fields, because even after the war, men remained in service. The land army had been created during the war, due to shortage of manpower. Women worked in the fields, farmed, and tended livestock, performing all the tasks of men. They wore smart uniforms when off duty, beige jodhpurs and tall, shiny brown boots, looking like they were ready to go horseback riding. I was a city girl and didn't think that working in the fields was my first choice. Nursing didn't appeal to me either, in part because my aunt had suggested I try it. Since I didn't know how to bandage a finger, I felt nursing school would not be right for me.

Domestic work, on the other hand, was something I'd done for the past four years back in Poland, and though I certainly didn't plan on being a domestic all my life, I figured that I might be able to arrange my hours so that I could both work and go to school. Finding a job was easy since there was a great shortage of domestic help in those days. I wanted to be independent and make my own choices and I didn't want to ask my aunt for spending money.

I also thought of going to art school to study commercial art one day. I went with Aunt Eva to Leeds University for the interview and showed the art professor my small portfolio of paintings and drawings. He was quite frank with me. He said that I had some talent but was no genius, and I knew that. He did add that after training in commercial art for three years, I could become a competent artist. He hastened to add that if a man and a woman applied for the same commercial art position, the man would surely get the job, even if the female applicant were the better artist of the two.

Dismayed at the professor's frank assessment about the inequality among the sexes in the work force and not being able to afford the tuition, I decided on the spot to abandon my dreams of becoming an artist and take a job as a domestic, going to school in the evenings.

The family I worked for consisted of a husband, a wife, and an eighteen-year-old daughter, Zena. Zena and I were about the same age, but we lived a very different existence. Friday night was date night for Zena; she spent hours dressing, changing her clothing again and again, and picking out the right shade of nail polish. As she prepared herself, I occupied my time with polishing an antique sterling centerpiece on the dining table. It was a huge piece, decorated with birds, tree branches, and very intricate flowers. Nestled in its branches were crystal bowls to hold chocolates, nuts, and fruit. The piece was exquisite, but polishing its every nook and cranny on Friday nights was time-consuming and laborious. It made me see how different my life was compared to Zena's. I promised myself then, that if ever I became wealthy, I wouldn't buy any object of sterling silver, even if I had a maid. What a waste of my time on Friday nights! I wondered if I'd ever be free to do what I desired, free to go on dates or just read and relax or go to a movie. I really couldn't imagine how I'd deal with such a situation. I never experienced going with girlfriends to the pictures, never had dates, and had no girlfriends. I couldn't carry on a conversation.

In school, I signed up for shorthand and typing classes, as well as English and Russian. At that time, I was quite fluent in Russian, having learned it while under Russian occupation. I felt that the language might be useful in the future and needed some improvement.

I didn't do very well in shorthand or typing, because I had trouble understanding the instructions of my teachers, but I kept struggling and plugging along.

One day, my little Russian Jewish teacher asked if I had any friends my own age. I said no because I couldn't yet converse with English girls. She asked me if I'd liked to meet a Polish girl who had had similar experiences during the war as I had. I enthusiastically accepted her suggestion. The teacher invited both of us to tea the following Sunday and I looked forward to the meeting. Rose and I struck up a friendship almost at once, one that would last a long time, I was sure.

Rose was living with relatives, and like me, trying to learn English. She asked me how much longer I was going to perform domestic duties. "Didn't you do enough menial tasks during the war?" The answer was yes, but now it was different because I was paid for my services, and I was going to night school. She planned to go into nursing, but I told her, "Nursing is not for me." She told me that she had already been admitted at Leeds General Infirmary for nurses' training in a few weeks.

We spent a wonderful couple of hours speaking in Polish together, while our Russian hostess kept pouring more and more tea for us. As we were leaving, Rose looked up at me and said, "Of course, nursing is a very difficult course of study." That remark did it! As I rode home on the bus, I kept mulling over the implications of her offhanded remark. *Nursing isn't too hard for Rose, but it would be too hard for me?*

The next day, I traveled to Leeds General Infirmary, where Rose was registered for the nurses' training, to inquire at the nursing office about enrolling for the same course. They said they were very sorry, but the admissions were closed and I'd have to wait six more months for the beginning of the next course. As I was walking out of the hospital, I decided six months was too long a wait. I boarded another bus and rode to St. James' Hospital at the opposite end of the city. I didn't call for an appointment, nor did I ask if they needed more student nurses. I simply walked in to the matron's office and was greeted by an elegant lady.

"How might I help you, my dear?" she asked in her very British accent, inviting me to have a seat. I told her I wanted to enroll in nurses' training. Matron picked a letter from her desk and asked me to read it.

"Do you understand what you've read?" she asked. And when I said I had understood, she informed me that I'd been accepted into the next nurses' training class. The whole visit took fewer than ten minutes and I was going to start my training at St. James at the same time Rose would begin her training at LGI. The matron told me that the first three months all of the new student nurses had to go through pre-training. We'd work on wards, learn how to make hospital beds, tuck the sheets with hospital corners, rub patients' backs to prevent bedsores, bathe patients, change their nightgowns, feed helpless patients, give bedpans, and many other nursing chores. Then we would take an entrance exam consisting of some basic nursing, some English, and math. You couldn't fail the entrance exam. If you did, you were out. During the next three years, there would be other exams, which if you failed, you could take again and again, but the entrance exam you had to pass the first time.

I gave notice to the family I worked for and moved into the nurses' residence in spring 1947. The residence was like a college dorm and for the first time in my life, I lived with young women my own age and felt that I finally fit in. I loved the social life and having my own room. I was able to take as many showers as I pleased, given that hot water flowed at all times in the nurses' quarters. I made friends with several of my class-mates. And when nurses' training began in earnest, I knew that Rose and my aunt had been right—nursing was the right decision for me to make. Whenever I had free time, I visited my aunt and on occasion, the Benns and Rose.

After pre-training, during which we learned how to actually care for sick patients, I took the entrance exam. I passed with flying colors, even helping friends in arithmetic, division and multiplication of fractions. Here were young women, recently graduated from high school, who couldn't solve simple problems, but I remembered math very well from my own school days in Poland. We all passed our entrance exam. Now began the real work: three years of nurses' training.

I worked hard, studied hard, and enjoyed every moment of training. I am proud to say that I never failed a single exam, though nursing wasn't easy. We worked twelve-hour shifts at night, and eight-hour shifts during the day. Lectures occurred in the morning, but after long nights and little sleep, we'd sometimes fall asleep, listening to the lecturer.

The nurse in charge was called "Sister," but the title had nothing to do with nuns. Some of the sisters on the ward were very strict; others were easier to get along with. I became friendly with several nurses, despite my accent and pronunciations. We studied together, went to the movies and dancing together, occasionally vacationed together. We had discussions on many subjects, but they never asked me about my life in Poland or anything about my parents or family, nor did I offer any information about what had happened to them. I don't think they knew I was Jewish.

A new friend, Joyce, encouraged me to start smoking, which she said would help me to stay awake on long night shifts. It took some getting used to and made me sick a few times, but soon enough I was hooked. At first, friends supplied cigarettes, but later they told me I'd have to buy my own. We were always short of cash.

The first year student nurses were paid one pound ten schillings per month. (One pound equaled twenty shillings and one schilling equaled twelve pence. One pence corresponded more or less to one cent.) Part of the money had to be spent on black stockings, which we had to wear with our uniforms, and any other expenses, including sweets, vacations, entertainment, and cigarettes. Food, shoes, and clothing were still rationed at that time, but apart from having coupons for clothing or shoes, we still had to pay for these items. The uniforms, food, and lodging were provided by the hospital. Luckily, nurses were allowed to see some movies for free, and we took advantage of that privilege. Sometimes my girlfriends and I would go to a dance, popular on the weekends in every city. We'd dress up as well as we could on a budget and we'd go out in hopes of meeting nice young men. We had a pact that if we liked a particular young man who wanted to accompany us home to the hospital, we'd let each other know. However, if we didn't like our partner, we'd say that we'd promised to go back to the hospital with our girlfriends.

The second year we were paid two pounds, ten shillings per month, but that pay was still very small, leaving little room for luxuries. If one wanted to buy a radio, one had to pay a monthly subscription fee. (There were no commercials then on radio, which was why owners had to pay money each month.) I was the only nurse who'd saved enough money from my time working as a domestic to buy one and to afford the monthly fee. My room was jammed in the afternoons with other nurses who liked to listen to soap operas.

We were always hungry coming home from a movie or a dance in the evenings. On the way home, we'd stop at the fish and chips shop. It cost six pence (a half shilling) to buy fish and chips, wrapped in newspaper, sprinkled with salt and vinegar. Nothing tasted as good as that piece of fresh fish with its crunchy batter and chips. A tuppence (two cents), would buy chips only, not enough to fill an empty stomach, but on some evenings, it was all we had. Sometimes, we had no money left and we'd sneak into the hospital kitchen to scrounge for leftovers from the previous meal we'd missed.

We had to study a lot for the upcoming exams. Work on the wards was continuous and demanding with beds to be made, patients to be changed and bathed, medicines to be given, wounds to be dressed, and many other duties. All the nurses complained about conditions, including long hours—sixty hours per week—and very low pay after graduation. When on night duty in the hospital, we had to slice and butter bread for forty patients for breakfast, cook eggs and porridge, and brew tea. Then we had to serve breakfast, help patients on bed rest to wash themselves, make beds and give medicines, all from 6:00 a.m. to 8:00 a.m. We also had to write a report and give a report to the day shift. We learned a lot and worked hard. I have fond memories of my training and the lasting friendships I formed with several nurses, including Rose, who graduated from LGI at the same time as I graduated from St. James Hospital. In England, every nursing school started at the same time, all the exams were given at the same time, and all the graduations were at the same time. We graduated in 1949.

Graduation from St. James Nursing School, 1949
(Gerda bottom row, second from left)

LEAVING ENGLAND

My cousin, Zygmunt Schwarzer, miraculously survived the war. During an *akcja,* Zygmunt's parents and his sweetheart, Renia Spiegel,[12] hid in the attic of my Uncle Samuel Goliger's building at Moniuszki 10. Because my uncle was part of the *Judenrat*, he was allowed to live outside the ghetto in his old apartment. The Nazis didn't "find" their hiding place; it was probably hateful neighbors who reported them to the police. Mobile killing squads made up of SS special forces, *Einsatzgruppen*, took all three out into the street and shot them. In his own words, Zygmunt wrote "Three shots. Three lives lost! It happened last night at 10:30 p.m. Fate has decided to take my dearest ones away from me." Later on, he was loaded on a train bound for Auschwitz and later, Bergen-Belsen, the first camp liberated by the Americans.

Like many young survivors, he married shortly after liberation. His wife, Genia (Jean), was a Polish Jew whom he'd met in Feldafing, a Jewish displaced persons (DP) camp in Germany. Zygmunt studied medicine in Stuttgart. After completing his studies, he and his wife immigrated to the United States, settling in Brooklyn. He had to take additional training in New York to obtain an American medical license and to practice pediatrics. After finding each other at the war's end, we stayed in touch.

---

12 An account based on the translated diary of Renia Spiegel, "The Unforgotten" was published in the November 2018 issue of Smithsonian, written by Robin Shulman.

As much as I liked living in England, I had always had a secret wish to live in America, the kind of dream I didn't think I'd ever realize, like living on the moon. Because Zygmunt was himself a refugee, he was unable to apply for a visa for me. However, he managed to get one from a doctor he worked with at the hospital, a man willing to vouch for me and say he'd support me, so that I wouldn't be a burden on the United States government. Zygmunt had told his colleague that by the time I arrived in America, I'd be a registered nurse and self-sufficient. I never planned to ask him for any kind of support. Vouching for me, a total stranger, was more than generous, and I was deeply appreciative of his gesture.

During the war, getting such a document meant saving a person's life. Many European Jews wrote to American relatives during the war, begging them for that precious piece of paper, one that would save their lives, but sadly, many people believed their families were exaggerating the situation in Europe about the plight of the Jews; they also worried that if their relatives were to come to America, they'd be obligated to support them. And so they remained silent. Only after the war did they find out that there had been no exaggeration and with the smallest help, they might have saved a life.

After becoming a state registered nurse (SRN) at St. James Hospital, I moved to London in the spring of 1950 to get to know the city better and to be close to the American Embassy.

America.

America was a word that always carried a certain mystique for me, even when I was a small child. America, the land of milk and honey, where the streets were paved with gold! America, a land of wonder and beauty, a land of skyscrapers, a land so far away and impossible to attain, that all I could do was dream about it. People in Poland talked about America as the ultimate bliss, more fairytale than real.

What I knew about America was that it was a powerful country, a free country that I'd seen in Shirley Temple films while I lived in Przemyśl. While in nurses' training, I corresponded with a woman in New York City who had known my parents. She worked for a television studio and had sent me a parcel from New York that contained, among other gifts, a pair of nylons. I was the envy of all the nurses in the hospital, as nylon manufacturing was so new. That pair lasted a whole year without snagging or developing runs. Making such durable merchandise was bad business, and the manufacturers must have caught on to that idea. By the time I arrived in America, I was unable to find such nylons again. The kind of stockings I had to buy would last a day or two before developing runs, and I had to run out to buy a new pair.

Aunt Eveline had not been happy about my decision to move to London and certainly not to the United States. She wanted me to stay close to her, but I yearned to see the world. She'd argued that life both in London and in America was very expensive and that I'd fare better by staying in Leeds. Though I agreed with her about the higher cost of living, I also knew that nurses earned much higher salaries in the States than in England. The feelings I had leaving Poznań returned; I felt a bit guilty leaving Leeds and the Mantels,[13] but I made the decision to go to London.

I got a job at West Middlesex Hospital in London as a staff nurse. The nurses' quarters were situated on vast grounds sloping down to the Thames. The property had belonged to Lord Warkworth in the 19th century. Constructed of wood, the house had a wide, carved staircase leading upstairs to a floor that had been converted into small bedrooms for nurses.

The ground floor had a large living room, dining room, and several sitting rooms, each equipped with a fireplace. The kitchen and maids' quarters were on the lower level. We ate breakfast and evening meals in the dining room with its intricately carved walls and doors. Immaculately kept lawns and the large garden kept groundskeepers and gardeners fully occupied. Sometimes, when I was off duty during the day and it didn't rain, I'd spend time in the garden, sitting on the bench reading a book;

---

13   The Mantels moved to Munich before the war. With the rise of Nazism, they sent their oldest, Walter, to study in London. In 1938 they themselves decided to leave Germany, packing a single suitcase, claiming to the authorities that they were going to visit their son at the university in London. My aunt had brought her fur coat, but as the train reached the border, the German patrol took it, saying she wouldn't need it in England during summer and that she could pick it up at the border on the way back, knowing full well she would not return to Germany.

other times I'd walk down to the river to watch university students training for crew, rhythmically rowing sculls. As a home for nurses, it was quite luxurious and the grounds were spectacular. It took me a few minutes to reach the hospital by bus, and the bus service was very frequent.

My friends, Joyce Shackleton and June Lammas, moved to London at the same time as I did; they planned to train as midwives. We met often, visiting museums or going to the movies. London celebrated its first post-war Festival of Britain, which we frequented often since the exhibits were free and we were always short of cash.

Before I moved to London, I'd corresponded with the American Embassy by mail, but responses were slow in coming. A relatively small quota of Polish citizens was permitted entry into the U.S., yet many Poles wanted to leave Poland, given the difficult postwar living conditions under Communist rule. Because of quota status, it was hard to determine how long one had to wait for their number to come up. Every few weeks I went to the Embassy to check on how long it would take for me to receive my papers.

The Embassy office occupied a huge circular room with a round table in the center. Clerks sat at individual windows around the room, ready to answer questions. One day I approached a clerk, asking again about my quota status and the departure date. The clerk was neither interested nor well informed, saying she had no definitive answer. Disappointed, I left the window. As I approached the circular table, I noticed a young man having trouble reading the questions on a form. I found out that he was Polish and had little knowledge of the English language. I offered to help by asking him questions in Polish and answering them in English on the form. As we worked together, the clerk taking care of his case approached our table and asked how he was coming along with his form. I explained that I was helping him because we both spoke Polish. She then asked me why I was at the Embassy. I answered her that I too wanted to go to America and was wondering when my quota number would come up. I didn't tell her that I'd already talked to another clerk. She asked to see my papers, examined my passport, and said, "Since you haven't lived in England for a full five years, you can still apply for a visa as a Displaced Person rather than as a Polish citizen. If you'd lived here more than five years, you wouldn't be considered a DP any longer, but the DP quota is much larger than the Polish quota, so your chances of going will be far better." She then said that I'd hear from the Embassy soon.

Six weeks later, my visa came in the mail along with a notification that I was scheduled to leave England within a couple of weeks. I never saw the Polish man who'd struggled to fill out his application nor do I remember his name, but my stopping to help him was a lucky coincidence.

The Hebrew Immigration Aid Society (HIAS) paid for my passage to America by ocean liner. How HIAS found out that I had no money for the fare is a mystery, but I received the ticket to leave London the first week of July 1951 and enclosed was a fifty-dollar bill to get me started in America.

There wasn't much packing to do since I had few possessions, but I was told that I had to wear an evening gown for formal dinners on the ship, when passengers were invited to the Captain's table. Never in my wildest dreams did I anticipate such excitement. I said goodbye to my cousins Ludwik and Gideon Gottlieb. June and Joyce, my friends from St. James, met me for a farewell dinner and promised to stay in touch. I sailed on the S. S. Washington, sharing a cabin with a young Irish woman, recently divorced, who was headed to America to start a new life. We became friends. I also enjoyed the company of a young Israeli man, but we never saw each other after arriving in New York.

The sailing was pleasant, the ocean as smooth as glass, the days sunny and warm, but I wasn't feeling entirely well. I sat at a table with an American family of Irish descent, who were returning home after their first visit to Ireland. The husband, a high-ranking deputy, and his teenage son were both tall, strapping men who ordered steak at the first dinner. Simply hearing their selection made me queasy; I rose from my seat, quietly excused myself, and promptly left the table.

As appealing as the ship's menus were, I lived on dry toast, bits of lettuce, and tomatoes for the duration of the trip. I spent a great deal of time on deck, breathing the salty air, but I stayed away from the dining room until our last night's meal.

That evening, my Irish dinner partners suggested I chance a drink to celebrate our arriving in the States. I asked them to recommend a true American cocktail and the response was a Manhattan or a Pink Lady. I drank not one but two Manhattans that evening—the first and only time during the crossing that I was able to eat and enjoy an entire meal.

AMERICA

Ellis Island was hot and humid the morning we arrived, August 1, 1951. The Atlantic looked like a molten mirror. People stood on deck, straining their necks to catch a glimpse of the iconic Statue of Liberty in the distance, shrouded in mist. It was very hard to describe my complex feelings about arriving in the United States of America. On the one hand, I was thrilled beyond measure to finally be in this great country. On the other hand, I had never experienced such heat and humidity and was miserably uncomfortable, wondering how long I'd be kept on the ship and whether or not Zygmunt would be there to meet me. I was thinking of neither the future nor the past; I was just happy to see America in the distance. I had fifty dollars in my pocket and I knew it wouldn't last long. After all, Aunt Eveline had warned me that life in the States was expensive. My hopes and fears mixed with excitement, and I waited in a long line to process papers through customs. Unbeknownst to me, Zygmunt was waiting patiently, legally unable to meet me until I was standing on American soil.

When the legalities were complete, I met my cousin Zygmunt. He took a long look at me, smiled, and embraced me. He claimed my trunk, and we set off for Brooklyn. I was thrilled to see my one surviving cousin. Zygmunt was working in the hospital as an intern, while his wife Jean had a job in the stockroom at B. Altman's Department Store on Fifth Avenue; limited English prevented her from getting a sales clerk job. Because of their meager earnings, Jean didn't think they could afford a taxi fare from

Ellis Island. But Zygmunt told her that as the only other survivor in the family, I shouldn't be schlepping luggage on several subways in such terrible heat, and he wasn't going to scrimp on my first day in America. In our conversation, he didn't talk about his own experiences or family losses in the camps. It was obviously too painful a subject for him to discuss.

We drove through Manhattan and I twisted my neck every which way, looking up at the skyscrapers. He pointed out New York Hospital, a huge conglomeration of buildings on the East River. "That's where I want to work," I said, not realizing how many difficulties I would have to face before I could actually work there. Finally, we arrived at his home. Zygmunt and Jean lived in a tiny room with kitchenette on Hopkinson Avenue, its single window facing the street. Jean served lunch, telling me proudly that tuna salad was a very popular dish. I had never eaten tuna before and frankly didn't much care for it.

Zygmunt had rented a room for me at Mrs. Glicksman's apartment on the street nearby. Mrs. Glicksman was a sweet old Jewish woman, who earned extra income by renting out a couple of rooms in her apartment. Her other lodger was a young Polish woman, older than I was, quite religious, and always looking for a husband. A person known as a *Shadchan* arranged dates for religious girls. Every so often a man would come to the apartment, wanting to meet her. They'd go on a date, and the next day we would have to listen to how the date had gone, blow by blow.[14]

Many Jewish families occupied the section of Brooklyn where I lived. One advantage to my new location was that it was only a few blocks to the subway station. Gradually I learned my way around the town. I came to America with a great profession and little money to my name. I was optimistic that I was going to be successful and planned to buy a baby blue Cadillac since my salary would be much higher than it had been in England. Never mind that I didn't know how to drive or the money to buy it! Nor did I know about buying a car or anything else with just a down payment and monthly payments. Nor did I realize that one had to park their car and have a garage space. I didn't worry about these minutiae.

14   I don't know if she ever met her future husband, because I moved from Mrs. Glickman's after several months to be closer to the hospital where I worked.

All I wanted was a baby blue Cadillac and a convertible, to boot—like Hollywood actors had. A Cadillac carried a famous, poetic name that all foreigners were familiar with.

It was another beginning, but more struggles began, though I felt that all the new problems were surmountable; there was nothing I couldn't overcome in this wonderful country. Zygmunt had generously paid thirty dollars for my first month's rent. I had to find a job soon because my fifty dollars wouldn't last long. Nevertheless, I couldn't get a job in any hospital because I did not have a New York State license. There was no reciprocity between my British license and an American Registered Nurse (RN) diploma. I spent days trudging from small private hospitals in Brooklyn to large famous hospitals in Manhattan, but the answer was always the same. They wouldn't hire me without the proper license. The only job I could get was a job as a cleaning lady. I told myself that I was a trained nurse and I was determined to practice my profession. I'd done enough cleaning for others and now I was ready to practice nursing.

One day I tried another hospital, Brooklyn Jewish Hospital, where they offered me a job as an undergraduate RN. The nursing supervisor told me I needed to take certain classes in order to obtain a license and that I had to get it within one year. Until then, I'd work at the hospital as an undergraduate at a lower salary. I found this offer very satisfactory. But I immediately faced another problem when the supervisor asked if I had a high school diploma; without one, I couldn't apply for a license. I told her that the war had interrupted my high school education. "Well," she said, "You will have to take a high school equivalency exam in order to get a high school diploma." I also had to take extra courses in E.R. work, gynecology and delivery that New York State required. And that wasn't all. She said I must take English classes as well. I asked her why, since I could speak and understand English perfectly well. She said that I spoke with an accent and had to improve it. I didn't want to spend any more time on schooling, because there were only twenty-four hours in a day. As we were talking, I mentioned that I even dreamed in English.

That seemed to be the magic statement. "If you dream in English," she said, "then you don't have to take English classes."

A few months later, I took my high school equivalency exam at Erasmus Hall.[15] Within a year after that, I got my New York State license. I was happy, had made many friends, liked my work, and even managed to do a bit of traveling.

In the late fall of 1951, three girlfriends and I went on vacation to Florida for a couple of weeks. One of the girls was my cabin mate on S.S. Washington. We heard a lot about the fabulous Florida beaches but had little money; we certainly couldn't afford to stay in famous air-conditioned hotels or eat in air-conditioned restaurants. We rented a room in a motel, spending most of the day on Miami beaches and visiting cool hotel lobbies in the afternoons and evenings. Nighttime we dealt with mosquitoes in our hot, stuffy room. Because we had to watch our expenses, at least once a day, we'd stop at a deli for coffee, where they had a selection of free assorted rolls, pickles, and sauerkraut on the counters. We made a meal of that free food, while sipping on our ten-cent coffee. It was a very new experience for all of us.

In my first winter in New York, I skated in Rockefeller Plaza. All it involved was renting a pair of boots and skates, and then stepping onto the ice to skate to music. I wasn't sure I'd still remember how to skate, but it all came back to me after the first few minutes. Skating smack dab in the middle of Manhattan while the music was playing was an exhilarating experience. There I was, Gerda Krebs, a girl from Przemyśl, skating in Manhattan, like any other young American girl, skating while people watched! A strange young man skated up to me and asked me to skate with him. Imagine! I never in my wildest dreams could have imagined actually being in New York and skating and having so much fun.

I hadn't been on skis from 1938 until 1952. In England, there wasn't much snow and the mountains weren't suitable for skiing; besides, skiing was the last thing that I'd thought about and I couldn't afford the price of

---

15 Erasmus Hall High School is the same school from which Barbra Streisand graduated many years later.

ski equipment or expensive resorts. In 1953, I had the chance to go to the Laurentian Mountains near Montréal, Canada, with a nurse friend of mine called Frances. The mountains were cold and the snow could be icy in a time before down parkas were obtainable. My jacket was thin and despite the fact that I wore a warm sweater and layered it with warm underwear, I was still quite cold. Skiing down the mountain for the first time was really thrilling, as I thought I might have forgotten how to ski. But I could schuss, slalom, and stop in the middle of the run as I wished. It was like the old days, except that instead of climbing or using a rope tow to get to the top of the mountain, there were T-bars and ski lifts. Frances took lessons since she'd never skied before.

We went to ski in Canada several times and made new friends. Though she and I had different personalities, we complemented each other, so much so that we later became roommates, renting a one-bedroom apartment in a Manhattan brownstone. I did most of the cooking. When she got married, I had to find another roommate. Frances's husband suggested a girl as a new roommate for me, but we turned out to be incompatible. The girl's mother kept calling, asking me to find dates for her daughter. I tried at first and arranged for double dates, but the guys never called her again. I felt sorry for her, but after trying a few times, I had to give up. Then there was sickness in her family and she had to go back home. I started looking for a less expensive apartment and decided against looking for another roommate. I was ready for more privacy and for being my own boss in my own place. I found a one-room apartment on York Avenue at 99th Street. I purchased a sleeping couch, a table and chairs, a chest of drawers, pots, pans, dishes, as well as linens. I was in business.

Life was wonderful. I rarely talked about my past or my family. No one wanted to hear about it, and I just wanted to get on with life. No one could understand how the Nazis had brutalized and murdered Jews. Perhaps they were not ready to hear the stories of survivors. I saw Jean and Zygmunt when they came to Manhattan. Zygmunt had finally completed all the medical requirements and opened a pediatric practice in his new home in Queens. He became a successful doctor, trusted and liked by his patients.

I worked in many hospitals. I also did private duty and worked on the staff at the New York Hospital and Mount Sinai Hospital on Fifth Avenue and 105th Street.

It was at Mount Sinai that I met Harold Seifer, a resident physician who was completing his medical training. One day he overheard me speaking, liked my accent, and asked me out for a date. At that time, I was dating a few young men and I had to juggle everyone's personality and whims, finding it rather trying.

Within a single week, Harold and I had three dates. Our first date was a walk around the governor's mansion, close to where I lived. Afterwards, we had coffee and cake in my apartment. Harold lived on a very tight budget and not knowing if he'd like me, he didn't want to spend or perhaps waste any of his cash. On our second date, we went to the movies. When I told Harold that I'd like to go upstairs to watch the film, he asked why. I answered that I could smoke upstairs. He then asked if I was addicted to cigarettes. " Oh no," I said, so we sat downstairs. During the course of the film, though, I went to the bathroom twice for a few puffs of a cigarette. I realized that I was unable to sit for two hours straight without lighting a cigarette. Harold was probably right—smoking had become an addiction, but it didn't stop him from dating me.[16]

We went out to dinner on our third date. In those days, the residents got a very measly salary of $60 a month, which had to cover car expenses, entertainment, and clothing. Once or twice a month, we went to a restaurant; other times, I was delighted to cook dinner for both of us. I loved cooking different dishes, and Harold enjoyed loved almost everything I prepared. The old adage turned out to be true: the way to a man's heart is through his stomach! Since I had more money than he did, I'd buy tickets for a theater, concert, or an opera. For one thing, he was the first person since I'd left Poland who wanted to know what happened during

---

16   When our first child Elizabeth was about five, she told me after I kissed her, "Mummy your breath smells." That was the first time I realized how my smoking affected other people. Later, I gave up the habit.

the war. Not only was he interested in history, but he also wanted to hear information from someone who had survived. Soon I was dating Harold exclusively. It all happened quickly and effortlessly. He was willing to try a lot of new experiences, including eating snails, attending opera, and skiing. After I gave him his first skiing lesson, I told him to take private lessons, since my instructions didn't carry much weight. On the other hand, Harold taught me to drive. I can't say that was a fun experience either, but I did learn, becoming a good and confident driver, and I wasn't afraid of freeways.

On May 29, 1955, in a rabbi's study in Manhattan, Harold and I were married. Since neither of us had the money for a big wedding, we kept it small and simple. I wore a blue suit with a matching hat. After the ceremony, we hosted a dinner at Tavern on the Green. Present were Harold's family, cousin Zygmunt and his wife, Jean. I was quite nervous, as the people who surrounded me were mostly strangers. There was no pomp or excitement, no wedding toasts or speeches, no dancing or photographer.

The next night we went to the theater, because I'd bought tickets for a Broadway show long before I knew we'd set a date to be married. The following day, we borrowed Harold's father's old Chevy and drove north to Canada. We spent a few days in Montréal.

The most memorable meal on our first evening in Montréal was at a French restaurant recommended by the hotel. The waiter suggested a rather expensive wine, and since neither of us was terribly knowledgeable or sophisticated about wines, we ordered it. The dinner was great and I was so full that I couldn't consider eating another bite, but then I saw Napoleons on the menu. I said to Harold, "I've got to have one." I couldn't resist my favorite pastry, so I ordered it.

The fluffy square arrived, covered with powdered sugar, layers of thin pastries and the most delicate vanilla crème filling in the middle. It was the first time since my childhood that I'd tasted anything that began to resemble my mother's kremówki. Eating something so familiar on my honeymoon gave that evening a special meaning. Since then, when I talk or compare this pastry with the Canadian Napoleon, I think of Mamusia and our honeymoon. I know I'll never taste this pastry as delicious as my mother's or the one in Montréal, but thinking about it brings a warm memory.

After several days in Montréal visiting museums, parks, and sights of interest, we drove north and then it was time to return to New York. I packed my belongings on York Avenue, and our life in Boston began in a one-room apartment in Brookline. Harold scheduled a residency at the V.A. Hospital. Once again, I had to work as an undergraduate nurse, because the state of Massachusetts claimed that their standard of nursing was higher than that of New York State and, therefore, my New York State license would not be recognized. Nurses who'd trained in the United States received reciprocity from one state to another, but my New York state license was only good in the state of New York. I worked mostly at Boston Lying Inn Hospital and Massachusetts General Hospital, again at a lower salary, since I was treated as an undergraduate.

Boston was hit hard by the polio epidemic in the summer of 1955. I was working at Mass General Hospital, taking care of polio patients during that hot, humid summer; there was no air-conditioning then. Nurses were required to wear double coats over uniforms and masks. When we left the ward, we took off both coats so as not to spread the disease to other parts of the hospital. Putting in eight hours in a polio ward was the hardest work I'd done in a hospital since nurse's training. My supervisors did not trust my judgment and looked down on me because I hadn't been trained in Massachusetts, a prejudice that extended to anyone who hadn't trained there. And yet, there were many Boston-trained nurses who refused to work with polio patients, fearful of catching the disease. Some evenings when I went home, my neck ached, and I was sure I had early symptoms of polio. Luckily, I avoided catching the disease despite helping those who were very ill.

Living in Boston gave me a chance to know Harold's parents and some of his relatives. His father, Joe, was a nice man, quiet and non-argumentative. His mother, Esther, was the matriarch who made all the decisions. She and Joe hadn't had an easy life, but they raised four boys, and always stressed education for their children. Melvin, the oldest, was charming and kind. Both he and Harold had attended Boston Latin High School and Harvard College. After college, Mel attended Harvard Law School, while Harold went to Tuft's Medical School. Twin boys followed. Maurice went to Lowell Technical School to study chemicals and textiles, and Frank died at the age of twenty, while still in college.

Harold's family didn't seem interested in learning about what happened to my family. I think that his parents and other people were uncomfortable to ask about my accent, where I'd come from, and why I'd emigrated. Perhaps they didn't want to hear gruesome tales about living through the Holocaust or yet another "far-fetched" account of what happened in Europe during the war.

Esther, my mother-in-law-to-be, continued to ask Harold if I was "really Jewish," since I didn't speak Yiddish. I found her question rather funny, if not a little bit insulting. Having gone through the Holocaust and having lost most of my family, I didn't need to prove to anyone that I was Jewish. After she got to know me better, Esther, or Grandma, as we called her, stopped asking these questions.

Harold wanted to finish his training in California at the V.A. Hospital in Long Beach. I was pleased that we'd be leaving Massachusetts and looked forward to living for a year in California. I had heard many positive stories about California and truthfully I wasn't happy living in Boston. I found Bostonians rather snobbish, and the salaries were lower than those of New York. More than that, the humidity really bothered me. Harold's mother wasn't too happy that we were leaving Boston. She was looking so much forward to bragging to friends about her brilliant son, the doctor, but she knew we were leaving Boston for only one year and that we'd be back to open the office in the city.

We purchased a new blue Chevrolet (not a Cadillac!) and left Boston at the end of June 1956. A moving truck picked up our few pieces of furniture, which I'd had since my single days. What I loved most about Boston was broiled lobster. Also, I loved the Boston symphony, summer concerts, and the evening art classes I took at Harvard. Boston is a city with a rich history that is the home to great schools and universities; nevertheless, I was glad we were leaving for a long cross-country drive and new adventures. We planned to do some sightseeing as we drove across the country.

Our car didn't have air conditioning—few cars did in those days—but it had an automatic shift. Driving through Arizona and Nevada in the early summer was sweltering. We drove across flat Kansas planes and up through the mountains of Colorado, where patches of snow were still on the ground in July. We visited the breathtaking Grand Canyon. Then we hit the Mojave Desert. We drove through the night to escape the higher temperatures in the sun, but the heat in the car was still unbearable. We wondered how large the desert could be and how far it stretched out.

And then, in the early hours of the morning, as we entered San Bernardino, the temperature suddenly changed. Cool, dry air blew in through the open windows. The difference in temperature was such a relief. We pulled to the side of the road, parked against a curb, and quickly fell asleep. We woke up refreshed about 6:00 a.m. We were in California! It took us about two more hours of driving before we arrived in Long Beach. We hit tremendous traffic on Lakewood Boulevard, where workers were arriving at Douglas Aircraft, manufacturer of airplanes.

There were many ads for jobs. One could just walk in and be hired on the spot. We drove to downtown Long Beach seeking a motel where we could just go to sleep, but the only rooms available were for vacation stays. Long Beach was a resort town during July and August. The motels were situated on the beach, and you couldn't rent a room for less than a week.

The sand was clear, and the beach was long and uncrowded, unlike the beaches on the East Coast. Eventually, we found a commercial motel, lay down on the bed, and fell fast asleep. When we awoke in the early afternoon, we took out a map of Long Beach and began looking for an apartment. It didn't take long to find a one-bedroom with a living room and kitchen at a reasonable price, three streets from the beach. In comparison to Boston, prices in California were much lower.

We liked our new apartment, and it was not far from the V.A. Hospital. It was a luxury to have a bedroom, because in Boston we'd had only one room that served as a bedroom, living room, and kitchen at nearly double the cost of what we paid in Long Beach for three rooms. Our furniture and luggage arrived the next day, and I started fixing our new apartment. The weather was sunny and dry, with no humidity or rain. Every morning the sky was overcast and we were sure it would rain, but by eleven o'clock in the morning, the sun came out. What's more, every day was just the same—a delight! Long Beach had a close-knit Jewish community as well as other supportive groups, such as the PTA and hospital volunteer groups.

Each time I took a walk in Long Beach, I saw the calm blue ocean. Palm trees seemed to be everywhere. I called the tall, skinny palms "the old ladies" with their stockings falling down their legs, the old dried lower leaves showing beneath fresh green leaves. Other palms looked like pineapples, plump and green, and others that had long beards, like those found in Palm Springs.

A few days after our arrival, Harold started working at the VA Hospital and I began getting to know Long Beach, a fairly large city, thirty minutes south of Los Angeles, depending on traffic. I looked for a job in a hospital and once again faced a familiar dilemma: California would not reciprocate my New York State license. And so I began working per diem as a private duty nurse. In time, I would work for other doctors in private offices. At the end of a year, Harold thought about staying in California and opening an office in Lakewood. It was easier to open a new practice in California than in Boston, where there were many well-known and established doctors. Harold's mother was very disappointed, but after many telephone conversations with her and a trip to Boston (when I was five months pregnant), our decision to stay in California was made. I was happy not to have to return to the East Coast, but I left the final decisions to Harold. He, of course, knew how I felt.

Harold opened an office in Lakewood in the summer of 1957 for the practice of internal medicine. I was his nurse. Elizabeth Jan was born on October 6, 1957. In the mornings, Harold worked at the V.A. Hospital,

I took care of the baby, cooked our evening meals, did the laundry (diapers included) and cleaned our apartment. When Harold returned from the V.A., the baby and I were ready to go to Lakewood to the new office. A patient loaned us a crib, which we put in an empty room in the office. For five or six months, Liz slept most of the time and didn't disturb us. Once she got older and required less sleep, I needed to spend more time with her and had to give up working in the office. Also, I was pregnant again. Philip Henry was born on March 31, 1959. We hired someone for the front office, and I stayed home with the children. We purchased a small house with three bedrooms, two bathrooms, and a good-sized backyard. When our daughter Elizabeth was three, I helped to start a nursery school at the Jewish Center with Lois Cohn, a retired teacher. The school met once a week for just a half a day, a modest beginning.

I became a frequent Jewish Community Center attendee, what with picking up my children from nursery school, attending organizational meetings, taking my children to swimming lessons, and going to exercise classes. I served as chairperson of the women's group of the UJA, as well as on other JCC boards in the summer of 1962.

In the early 1970's I got a call from Sharon Kenigsberg, Director of Community Development at JCC. Sharon asked me to speak at The National Council of Jewish Women because they couldn't afford to pay a speaker. Sharon asked, "Have you ever given a talk about your experiences as a Holocaust survivor?" At first I was dumbfounded, never having been asked that question, but finally I mumbled that I'd give it a try, though she shouldn't expect me to talk like a professional. She was relieved when I said yes. She told me that I'd do "just great."

By the day of the meeting, I still didn't know exactly what I was going to say. When I entered the meeting room and was introduced, however, I began talking on a subject that was very familiar. My speech was not well organized nor was I a skilled speaker. It didn't seem to matter, since I held the attention of the whole room, or nearly the whole room. Some women sitting at a nearby table seemed to be having their own discussion about the sale of tickets for a future event—very unnerving.

Still, my audience gave me a round of applause when I finished speaking, tears were shed, and I received many nice comments. From then on I also started speaking in junior and high schools.

In 1985, the Board of Education required California schools to include in their curriculum the study of the Holocaust, but while talking to students, I learned that their teachers were themselves uneducated on the subject. Slowly, knowledge of this great tragedy started seeping into schools, and many teachers wanted to know more. After my first talk at JCC, I began speaking regularly to countless students, organizations, policemen—to anyone who wanted to hear my personal account. I spoke at schools even while on vacation. I spoke to audiences in Poland, England, and many states across the country, never tiring of telling my story. I spoke at Holocaust museums. I had a good rapport with my audience, talking *to* them and not *at* them; many would remember some of my personal stories and that was what mattered most to me.

Harold and Gerda, Wedding Day 1955

AMERICA

Harold and Gerda on skis in front of the Matterhorn, Zermatt, Switzerland, 1972

The Seifer children, Liz, Philip, and Julia in the late 1990s

Harold and Gerda at the Memorial dedication to her parents,
outside the Jewish Community Center in Long Beach, 2014

Harold and Gerda attending a Teachers' Workshop at CSULB

Gerda speaking to a senior class in 2016

FIRST RETURN TO POLAND

Harold and I planned to ski in Switzerland with a group of doctors in 1972. Harold also wanted to see Poland, the country where it "all happened," so we shortened our ski time to one week, planning on a week to visit Poland. I wasn't happy about going back to a country where I'd lost my family and experienced so many traumas. Frankly, I was afraid of Communist Poland, but I had agreed to go. We got our visas, and after a week of skiing in Switzerland, we flew from Zurich to Warsaw.

We flew on the Polish airline, Lot. The plane was filled with mostly men, all of them dressed in drab black suits, coats, and hats. There was no happy relaxed conversation going on. Each passenger seemed engrossed in his own private thoughts and remained quiet. Once the plane arrived in Warsaw, the passengers walked out in an orderly fashion, their faces without expression. It seemed as if eyes were looking at us from everywhere.

As we entered the airport, we were paged over the loudspeaker. Who knew our names? Who wanted us? I became nervous because we were back under a Communist regime I'd already experienced. A beady-eyed man approached us from Orbis Travel Agency who had our train tickets to Przemyśl. I gave him the name of the Bristol Hotel we'd tried to book, but he categorically told us that we did not want to stay there but at the Hotel Europejski. It turned out that he knew all about our travel plans, and when I asked him why Orbis hadn't answered any of my letters, he simply said, "we never write back." He was hoping to stay with us for the whole week, but I told him that I spoke Polish and wouldn't be requiring his assistance. He demanded a bottle of liquor as a bribe before he'd give us our railroad tickets that he held tightly in his hands. In every airport there was a foreign goods store where you could obtain cigarettes, liquor, chocolates, and other luxury items with foreign currency only. Harold bought a bottle of liquor and we exchanged it for the two railroad tickets. Little did I know that I could've obtained these tickets simply by going to the railroad station and buying them at the ticket window! The man drove us to the hotel. We got out of the car and never had to deal with him again.

To our great surprise, Janina Tarasiukowa greeted us in the lobby of the hotel. I had written her, telling her when we planned to visit Poland, nothing more, but she had apparently found out which hotel we were staying in. She was craftier than a CIA agent! It was the first time Harold met her. I had told him a lot about her, and he found my descriptions very much on target. Of course, they were unable to talk because neither spoke the other's language. I was their interpreter. I gave Janina the many gifts we'd brought for her, and she invited us for dinner on another day.

Registering at the hotel meant leaving our passports at the desk. While Harold was taking care of the registration, a young woman sitting at another desk looked at me and put her finger to her mouth, gesturing to me with a smile not to talk anywhere in the hotel. When Harold finished registering, I suggested we walk up the stairs to our room rather than take an elevator. He asked why. I told him what the young clerk had insinuated. He didn't believe me and thought I was imagining the whole thing. But I insisted that we had to be careful with what we said and that we should write each other little notes rather than talk in the room. On each floor of the hotel, an old woman sat at a small table, whose main duty was watching the comings and goings of the guests. She always had a cup of tea at her side and noted when the guests came and left the room. I had heard reports of guests whose suitcases had been searched, but I don't think ours had been.

We went to Tarasiukowa's apartment, where she lived with her married children in a three-bedroom apartment. A large room served as both living and dining room. It was quite a crowd inside the tiny apartment, but it was normal in those days. We were served a soup made of cow's stomach that Harold actually enjoyed, though he'd never tasted it before. "Baby Andrew" sat at the table with his wife and their little girl. My gifts, which filled one big suitcase, consisted of coffee, cartons of cigarettes, jeans, and other clothing—all requested by Janina.

From Warsaw, we took a train to Przemyśl. Nearing the railroad station gave me palpitations. Suddenly I was very nervous, excited, and actually curious to see it after an absence of thirty-two years. Once we left the station, all the street names were familiar, as if I had left Przemyśl yesterday. Yes, there were some bombed out buildings, a few new structures, but on the whole, the city looked as it did in 1940. I showed Harold my mother's building where I'd grown up. Before the war eight families had lived in eight apartments, but by 1972, there were eighteen tiny apartments; people were allowed only a certain amount of square feet per person. Therefore, if a member of the family moved or died, one room of that apartment was separated by a thin wall, a new door was made to the single room, and a new quarter was created to fit one or two people. The toilets were still outside, and the new occupants put in a single gas burner for cooking; if they were lucky, they could get a water faucet rather than having to fetch a bucket of water from outside.

We walked to 10 Moniuszki Street where my uncle Samuel Goliger's large building stood. It was two stories high, consisted of twenty or more apartments, and was built in a square, surrounding a large yard. A balcony facing the yard ran all along the building with doors leading to each apartment. The house looked well cared for. Since my uncle hadn't claimed his house, the city government had taken it over and sold individual apartments. Of course, I could have claimed the house as my own, but with some people owning their apartments, it would have been impossible to prove my right to the building.

My mother's house, in contrast to my uncle's, was neglected, its walls crumbling, the brass door handles dirty and dull, and many windows were broken. It gave me a very sad feeling. The backyard, which used to have a nice garden, was bare; there were no flowerbeds or trees. A woman peered out the window and I told her that I used to live in that apartment. "Could we come and take a look at it?" She was pleasant and let us in. I asked her if by any chance she might have found any doll or toy that might have been left there from my childhood. Unfortunately, she'd found nothing. Other families had lived in the apartment before she'd moved in.

Upstairs, we knocked at an apartment door that was occupied by the Męcinski family. Pani Męcinska opened the door. She recognized me immediately, hugged and kissed me and invited us inside for tea and cake. Her sister and her niece, Eva Sokoluk, joined us. We talked about pre-war days. Naturally, we spoke Polish, and my poor husband had to sit through our conversation, not understanding a word. The three ladies were so happy to see me and were very welcoming. I have heard stories where survivors came back to see their homes or apartments and were not allowed to enter and were treated very badly. Some of those neighbors would say things like, "What, you're still alive? Hitler didn't finish you all off?" Happily, that had not been my experience.

Afterward, we went to the center of the city. I showed Harold St. Hedwig's, the elementary school I'd attended, the park where I'd played, the street where my father's store had been—now occupied by a food store with little stock on the shelves.

We went to Przemyśl City Hall and found that my mother's house listed me as the heir of the building, but the lumberyard, which had belonged to my uncles, Adolf and Henryk, had been taken over by a travel agency, Gromada, that had plans to build a hotel on the huge lot.

As we walked in the city, many unimportant and very important events suddenly filled my head. As Przemyśl was close to the Russian border, it had few visitors, especially foreigners. Dressed like foreigners and suntanned in winter from skiing in Switzerland, we stood out wherever we went. If we looked at a shop window, pedestrians would stop and gape at us. When we looked at them, they turned their heads in embarrassment. Many people had never seen people so well dressed. I wore a sealskin ski jacket, and Harold wore a long sheepskin coat. We found a restaurant near the rail station, which I remembered from before the war. It was quite crowded, and as we entered, everyone sitting at the tables turned their heads in our direction. Diners sitting close to us were even more surprised, hearing me speaking Polish, ordering dinner. The food was extremely inexpensive when paid with dollars. Everything that the restaurant offered was tasty. We exchanged dollars into zloty, getting thirty zloty for one dollar. However, in a black market, people would come up to us and offer 600 zloty for a dollar. People could buy luxury items in foreign stores, but they had to have U.S., English, or German currency. Polish stores had few supplies and those were of poor quality. However, there were stores selling Polish handmade wares, such as carved wooden boxes and figurines, as well as amber jewelry that was set in steel (silver and gold were not available then). But the best items the shops had to offer were handcrafted wool rugs, decorative pillow covers, table and chair covers, and beautiful wall hangings.

After this short visit in Przemyśl, we took a train to Kraków, a beautiful old city at the foot of the Carpathian Mountains. Kraków was lucky to be spared destruction as the Nazis retreated from the city. It had become a UNESCO world heritage city. Everywhere we went, we felt the Communist influence because the people were not open and were afraid to speak their minds.

The next day, we took a taxi to Auschwitz and spent four hours going from one building to another, looking at photographs, crying at brutally committed murders there during the war. There are pictures of children with shaved heads, frightened little children with tears in their eyes, naked children who could barely stand, their ribs protruding in starved bodies. I looked at these pictures thinking, "what if those children were my children?" We saw the gas chambers and the ovens where the bodies were burned. It is hard to describe all that we saw and harder still to describe how we felt about Auschwitz and what went on there, while the rest of the world looked the other way. I remember the brick wall against which victims had been shot. I remember a display of a variety of hair types that had been shaved: long, short, braided, blonde, brown, and many shades of gray. There were windows with displays of all kinds of shoes and another with eyeglasses and combs and suitcases with names and addresses of the many thousands of victims. Auschwitz gives one all the information about cruelty and torture that the Nazis inflicted on those who were about to be shot or gassed or burned in the ovens. On the way back in a taxi, we were silent; there were no more tears left, no more words to describe the atrocities committed, man's inhumanity to man, the bestiality and complete lack of any guilt on the part of the murderers. I'm glad we went back to Poland, I'm glad I saw my town, and painful as it was, I wouldn't have missed the experience of going through Auschwitz. I was grateful that I had not been one of its victims, as many of my closest relatives were. It was a grim and painful memorial to the more than a million Jews, Poles, and Roma murdered there. At the time we visited, Auschwitz had not become the major tourist destination it is today; thus there was little information upon entering and no guidebooks. Harold and I traveled there three more times, taking one of our children with us each time. By then, there were many more visitors, guidebooks, and long lines. On our last visit, there were kiosks that sold postcards and books, as well as a snack bar. It looked more like Disneyland than an encampment whose purpose was the wholesale massacre of European Jewry. Children, accompanying their families happily played hide and seek, totally unaware of what had taken place within the camp. By the grace of God, they were living in a time when they would not be starved, beaten, or forced to undergo sadistic medical experiments. In those years, few people asked survivors about their experiences, how they had survived, or what had happened to their families. People just did not ask such questions, and survivors were not forthcoming with their stories.

We left Poland, stopping in England to visit our relatives, grateful to be in a free country again. What a different feeling to see throngs of happy, smiling, colorful people!

ANKA PIPER

Anka survived the war and sometime in 1980s, long after I'd moved to America, I attended a meeting of The Children of The Holocaust, of which I am a member. There I met a man from England who happened to be Anka's cousin. He told me that she was living in Israel. He gave me her address and I wrote to her in Polish, saying, "You survived and I survived! What are you doing now?" In her return letter, she said she hated the Polish language and would rather I wrote to her in English, because she was able to write in English to a degree. Since I wasn't able to write Hebrew, I was glad to correspond with her in English; by then it was easier for me to write in English than in Polish.

Anka wrote back, saying that after the war she'd married a man much older than herself and that they had had two sons. They eventually divorced, and she was living on a kibbutz. For a time, we wrote back and forth, but after a while, we stopped.

Years later on a trip to Israel, I found her phone number and called her. She was still living in the kibbutz. Her first sentence to me was, "How did you get my phone number?"

"I'm in Israel, I'd love to see you," I said.

"No, that's impossible," she said.

We'd rented a car, so I offered to come to her, but she was very adamant about not being able to see me under any circumstances.

Harold thought she may have been embarrassed about her lifestyle. She sounded very depressed. I was sorry we couldn't meet her because we'd been the only two Jewish students in *Gimnazjum* in Przemyśl and we'd both survived.

We didn't see her then or any other time. She just wished us a nice time in Israel. Our correspondence stopped after that, and I was disappointed; meeting someone from my past would have meant a lot to me. I had hoped she might feel the same.

LETTER FROM EVA SOKOLUK

Eva Sokoluk's family, Męciński, lived in our building before the war in an apartment above ours. After the war and after her aunts had died, Eva, a retired school teacher, was the only occupant in the apartment, which by then had one bedroom/living room, kitchen and bathroom. Even though I had sold the building several years earlier, I insisted that her rent should never be raised; we actually paid the new owner to install a tub in her bathroom. We saw Eva on each trip, brought her gifts, and took her out to restaurants, because it was a special treat for her. Eva lived a simple life on her retirement allowance, watching every *grosz*—penny. Unfortunately, on our last trip, she was unable to walk down a flight of stairs to see us and I couldn't walk upstairs. She looked down at me from her window; I stood on the street, looking up at her, and we exchanged just a few words.

A few years earlier in 2002 or 2003, I had received a letter from Eva that made a great impression on me. It contained part of an article written by Anna Strońska about her aunt who used to take her shopping when she was a little girl to my father's store. She went on at great length about the store, bringing back many childhood memories for me.

Several years ago on a visit to Przemyśl, I had seen in an antique store a very attractive painting of a little girl holding a teddy bear. I wanted to buy it. The painter was Marian Stroński, an artist from Przemyśl. I found out that his daughter, Anna, the little girl in the painting, was still living in town. We asked at the antique store if we might meet Anna, and they said she worked at the library, which had once been an old synagogue—the only synagogue not destroyed by the Nazis. We knew well the building's location as we had passed by it many times, wondering what it looked like inside.

We met Anna at the library and arranged to meet at her home after she finished work. I wanted to see her father's other paintings, still in her possession. She told us that she would show us the pieces but wouldn't sell them. Subsequently, I did buy the painting from the antique shop, because it was charming. Since we had time on our hands, we went to the city museum where we saw quite a few of Marian Stroński's paintings. He had been a prolific artist who'd painted all his life and had even managed to sell enough of his work during the war to support his family. He painted both portraits and landscapes. His styles varied, but I liked all the paintings we saw. I also bought a book of his paintings.

That evening, we went to Anna's home. She was married to a local artist, but from the appearance of the house they seemed quite poor. It was a huge, sprawling house, which had belonged to her family and must have been beautiful at one time. It stood high on a very steep and narrow street near Zamek. As we entered, the smell of cat urine was strong throughout the house. Cats were everywhere on the furniture, on the table, the upholstery had been shredded, and the floors were dirty. Anna offered us tea, and though I wasn't certain how clean the cups were, we accepted the drink to be polite.

She showed us a few paintings and among them was a watercolor of a tower, which reminded me of the Fredreum Tower in the park. I told her I'd like to buy it. She talked it over with her husband and came to the conclusion that though she was reluctant to sell any of her father's art, their roof needed repair and they needed money for the project. They decided to let us buy the watercolor. We then had two of Marian's paintings, one a watercolor, the other an oil. Anna told us a bit about her father and her childhood. She remembered specifically when her father had painted her, so owning the painting and meeting the model was icing on the cake. All the while we talked, Anna smoked one cigarette after another and coughed a typical smoker's cough.

Two years later, we went to Przemyśl again. We went to the library to see Anna, but another librarian informed us that Anna had died of lung cancer. We were shocked. Though only in her forties, she'd been a chain smoker. Her husband remarried soon after her death, and no one knew the current owners of her large, rambling house. Again we went to the antique shop, where there were two more paintings by Stroński. This particular antique shop had a narrow room that was always cold and crammed with knick-knacks, icons, furniture, broken and chipped pottery, dusty old books, bits of cloth and lace, silver and jewelry, and one wall crowded with old photographs and paintings. It was hard to get close to the wall as the light was very poor. The shop had no electricity, probably because it was part of an old passageway. We asked to have a painting taken down so we could see it in the daylight. The painting was of a fisherman in a boat on the lake and seemed peaceful, reminding me of the American artist, Winslow Homer.

We bought the painting, though it cost more than it should have, since the owner of the store knew us by then.

Going back to Eva's letter, she enclosed a copy of an article from *Sennik Galicjanski*, a title that translates as a Sleepy Galician, but it is also the name of a pamphlet. In the article, Anna muses about her childhood in Przemyśl. She mentions visits to a dentist who accepted Stroński's paintings for his services. She also wrote about her mother and aunt shopping for fabrics at the Krebs store. She wrote that selecting fabrics was a very important task in those days. One needed to consider all possibilities, and my father treated his "special" customers with great delicacy and understanding, avoiding mention of the price of the fabric. The article says that my father was very patient with his customers, whispering to them to take their time and to extend their visit as long as they wished—as if his whole day was at their disposal. She said that he loved selling, loved telling them where the given fabric came from, how it was made, and how to clean or wash the garment. She does not exactly remember my father because she was just a little girl standing beside her aunt, but to her, the store was filled with multicolored silks, ribbons, chiffons, crêpe de chines and georgettes, all of the finest quality. The article brought me back to the days when I would go to the shop and be on my best behavior. After all, children were supposed to be seen and not heard in those days and could definitely not interfere with grownup business and conversation. Those were times when children knew their place and certainly did not dare to embarrass their parents with rude behavior.

My dear daddy. It was thrilling to discover how well his clients thought of him and how gallant he could be with them, and how much they trusted his taste and knowledge of fabrics.

I wish I had at least one photo of my father. I have just the memory of his photo when he was a handsome young student in *Gimnazjum*, wearing a velveteen uniform and holding his hat in his hand, blond wavy hair still growing on his head. He had a short little nose and always wore a smile on his face. He was not terribly tall by today's standards. He was chunky but muscular, a good swimmer and dancer, and a connoisseur of good food. He was my daddy.

PRZEMYŚL

During one of our trips to Przemyśl in the late 1990s, Harold, Julia, and I stayed at the Biały Orzeł, The White Eagle Hotel, on the same street where my house stood. While having breakfast in the hotel, we met three men in the dining room who were speaking English. It was a most unusual occurrence to hear English in Przemyśl at the time. For that matter, one saw very few foreigners in Przemyśl in those years. We asked the men what they were doing in the city. Two of them were businessmen from Canada, trying to help Poles start and develop businesses. The third man was a Pole who spoke fairly good English. He was the intermediary between the Canadians and Polish business people.

The Polish gentleman asked us what we were doing in Przemyśl. I told him that the house on Piłsudskiego Street had belonged to my parents and that I had lived there before the war. He became very excited, insisting that we meet his mother who lived on the other side of the River San. Though we were ready to leave Przemyśl after breakfast, we asked our driver to take us to the apartment of the young man's mother for a short visit.

The short visit turned into a long visit. First we were served tea and homemade apple cake. Then the woman told us a story.

Her grandmother's maiden name was Goliger (my mother's maiden name) and she'd married a Catholic. They lived in Przemyśl. I had never before heard her name mentioned. It must have been a family secret; as a child I'd known nothing about it. The woman said that during the Nazi occupation, her father had been arrested and interrogated several times by the Gestapo. The Nazis had considered her father Jewish (a second or third generation descendant of a Jew), and so her father was called into the police station several times for questioning. He was lucky to be released each time. On one such occasion, our hostess had gone with her father to the police. She was petrified of the Nazis. All the Gestapo members acted very scary, as if they were ready to kill or arrest you. She didn't see any maltreatment, but when they were finally released and allowed to leave the police station and go home, the young girl was so angry with her father that she beat him with her small fists, crying and asking why he had to have a Jewish relative, why he would have anything to do with Jews.

On the day she told us that story, she admitted that she felt actually more Jewish than Catholic, saying that since we were sort of related, she was very happy to have met me. She was about my age and we corresponded for a while. We saw her on another visit to Przemyśl, but she behaved rather oddly. It was hard to have a conversation with her. When we invited her to a restaurant, she didn't order any food but sat at the table, drinking tea and watching us eat. She didn't trust any food she hadn't cooked herself.

I knew nothing about my grandparents; I'd never met them nor asked my parents about them. And I didn't know the first name of the woman's grandmother. I don't know how religious my grandparents were, but it seems they did not want to consider her part of the Goliger family, given that she'd married a Catholic. She'd stopped existing for them. I wondered how many other family secrets I didn't know. I'll probably never know…

RETURN TO LWÓW

For years, I wanted to return to Lwów. Though the city had been part of Poland for 400 years and again following the end of the First World War, Lwów was declared part of an independent Ukraine in 1991. In 2002, Harold and I planned to visit Lwów. We called the Ukrainian embassy in Washington to obtain a visa. Unfortunately, the embassy does not answer their mail nor do they answer their phone. The situation became even more frustrating when I contacted the travel agency. We were told that we could obtain a visa, but it would take several weeks. We didn't have the time: we were leaving for Europe in two weeks. Furthermore, we would have had to send our passports to the travel agency, $100 dollars apiece, plus $50 for postage and another $100 dollars for their services.

"All of this for a two-day visa?" Harold asked.

Ultimately, he refused to put our passports in the mail for safety's sake. We had pretty much decided not to go, but then I had an inspiration. I contacted a professor who'd been managing the Jewish Cultural Center in Kraków. The professor returned my email, answering that he'd contact the Ukrainian embassy in Kraków to make an appointment for us to obtain visas in just a few hours. Sure enough, the day after our arrival in Kraków, we hurried to the embassy at 10:00 a.m., and after depositing cash of $200 dollars into a specific bank, we were given a visa, stamped into our passports.[17]

What was so important that I felt I had to visit Lwów? Perhaps I felt I had to see the Janowska Street camp or what was left of it. We don't hear much about that camp or about the Bełżec extermination camp, about the Piaski Mountain, about the Kleparów railroad station from which so many Jews were deported, about the railroad station where hundreds and thousands of Jews were sent to Bełżec to be gassed. How many people have now heard of these names? Many people have heard of Auschwitz, Bergen-Belsen, and Treblinka, but the names of the camps in Eastern Poland have been largely neglected and forgotten. That was why I had to go there once more: as a pilgrimage to the land where my parents had lived and where they'd been murdered

In the 1960s or 1970s, I learned more concrete information from a man, a Dr. Drix, who'd written a book about his experiences in Janowska Street Camp. The Nazis had built a sub-camp on the Janowska Street section of Lwów, where most victims were brought before going to Bełżec. The camp remained active until the end of the war and Dr. Drix had miraculously survived, working as a doctor at Janowska Street camp. After reading his book, I called him in New York, where he resided and still practiced medicine. I asked him if, by some unlikely chance, he had met my mother after she'd been rounded up from the ghetto. He answered, "My dear lady, my own mother and my sister were both taken during the same *akcja*. They had no chance of survival because they were taken straight to Bełżec extermination camp in Eastern Poland. No one survived Bełżec."

Bolek, our Polish driver had been to Lwów many times and knew the city fairly well and how to deal with the police at the border. We'd

---

17   A London friend related a similar story about the Polish ambassador in London who'd offered to get her a Ukrainian visa. After a few days, he called her quite embarrassed, relating that the Ukrainian embassy in London didn't answer their phones either.

heard stories of people having to wait for hours at the border, stories about having to pay bribes. Thus it came as a pleasant surprise to cross the border in less than an hour, without any questions or problems.

As soon as we were in Ukraine, the conditions of roads deteriorated. The houses and the people looked poor, neglected, and sad. We drove another hour and a half, at last entering the old cobblestone streets of Lwów. Before the war, Lwów had been considered a cosmopolitan city, famous for its opera house, university, museum, and wide boulevards. As we drove on, the streets were full of potholes, and the roads were narrower than I'd remembered. They really hadn't shrunk, but they could no longer accommodate automobiles, street carts, and hordes of people. Furthermore, there were few traffic lights, and most cars disregarded them anyway.

We checked into the Grand Hotel, located on the main boulevard leading to the opera house. The hotel was a pleasant surprise, nicely appointed, with prices equivalent to any large European hotel. It was early enough to explore the town. I was hoping to recognize the little house that my parents had rented before we were forced into the ghetto. Bolek took us to the only remaining synagogue in Lwów, an orthodox synagogue that was spared destruction because the Russians used it as a storage depot; the Germans had found it convenient for the same purpose. The synagogue could have used interior renovations but Hebrew writing was still visible on the walls, though the paint was chipped in places. It was a dark place with no proper altar, only folding tables and chairs; however, they did have a *minyan*, a quorum of ten men, who met every morning.

We met an old Ukrainian woman, who more or less ran the order of things and knew everybody and everything. In addition, there was a young girl who knew a smattering of English and was happy to use it on us. They helped us phone Sarah, the rabbi's wife or *rebbetzin*, to arrange a meeting with her the next morning. At first, I had trouble speaking with Sarah in Ukrainian, since I'd forgotten the Ukrainian language I'd studied in elementary school, and Sarah didn't speak Polish. As luck would have it, she spoke fluent English, because both she and her husband had come from Brooklyn. What a joy for both of us to be able to converse without using our hands!

Bolek told us that he had to find a garage that employed a watchman so he could sleep peacefully. If he left his car in the street during the night, there would have been little left of it by morning. We ate at an outdoor restaurant while Bolek paid two boys, ten and twelve years of age, to watch the car. He didn't even trust parking the car on a busy street in broad daylight. The boys told us that they needed money for their mother, because their father was unemployed and alcoholic. This sounded like a very familiar story.

The next morning, Sarah came to meet us at our hotel. She was a charming young woman with a cute face and the figure of a woman who'd borne six children in a short time span. She wore a *sheitel*, a wig worn by all observant married Jewish women. While her husband took care of the synagogue, Sarah was able to run a day school. Luckily she had many helpers who looked after her children and did all the housekeeping. Needless to say, with all of the unemployment in Ukraine, one could get a lot of help for a small amount of money. I asked why she and her husband had left America to come to Lwów. She answered simply that they were needed there and were doing a lot of good for children and families.

Our first stop was Janowska Street where the labor and transit camp had been during the war. All that was left of it was a quiet pond, surrounded by wild, lush trees and bushes, climbing as if trying to reach the sky. A handful of decades before, it had been a lake full of blood flowing from the murdered Jews on Piaski Mountain. The soil had become rich, the trees and bushes having flourished on the blood of innocents. There is a large rock, ringed by flowers, inscribed in Polish, Hebrew, and English:

Let the memory of all the Nazi genocide victims in Janowska Death Camp remain forever.

And in Ukrainian and English, a sign:

PASSER-BY, STOP!
BOW YOUR HEAD!
In front you see a spot of the former

Janowska death camp.

The ground is moaning.

Here the innocent victims

were tortured and tormented;

here they were executed

and sent to the gas chambers!

MAY THE MEMORY OF THE INNOCENTLY
MURDERED LIVE FOREVER!
ETERNAL MALEDICTION BE UPON
EXECUTIONERS!

Sarah told us that until recently, the police had trained dogs there for police work. Small buildings that housed the dogs still remained. The visitors to Janowska Street and camp had complained about barking and the disturbance to a sacred site, so eventually the dogs were removed. Nothing remained of the camp itself. One can only imagine the suffering, beatings, disease, and starvation that were the daily routines of the inmates.

Driving up Piaski Mountain was difficult, but I asked Bolek to try, hopefully without ruining his tires. Somehow he managed to get us to the top of the very steep and narrow road. Below us lay the grey buildings of a present-day jail. At the top, the ground was sandy, and there were a few broken-down railroad streetcars. A couple of men worked on the streetcars. Despite the area's brutal history, it was very quiet and peaceful on the hill. I asked the two Ukrainian workers if I could have some sand, and they willingly obliged, digging sand and putting it in a plastic bag for me.

The men said that digging sand for construction was forbidden because it was strewn with many human bones, though the Nazis had done their best to rid the area of bones by grinding them to dust in specially built drums and scattering them to the winds. One of the workers told us how every so often a group of religious Jews from the United States would climb or drive up the hill to pray. Some groups would bring food and cooking utensils and stay there several days, praying for murdered souls.

We drove back down to the street and then a bit farther. We came upon an insignificant little grey building, the railroad sub-station in Kleparów, a suburb of Lwów. Before the war it had been a substation of the central station. The Nazis, however, had used Kleparów Station for a different purpose. Empty cattle trains waited there day in and day out, only to be crammed with the innocent victims of German brutality. Part of Hitler's infamous plan was for a "Final Solution" to the "Jewish Question," and became known as Operation Reinhard—the systematic annihilation of Jews between German-occupied Poland and German-occupied Soviet Union. Jews were rounded up by the thousands, kicked and beaten, and shoved as fast as possible into cars so they could reach their destinations— the death camps of Chelmno, Bełżec, Sobibor, Treblinka, Auschwitz-Birkenau, and Majdanek.[18]

The Bełżec camp was designed in such a way that the train arrived alongside its wall. All the victims had to quickly disembark, undress, and have their heads shaved (the Nazis used the hair for stuffing mattresses). All clothing taken from "the dirty Jews" or *Untermenschen* was washed and sent to Germany, so that pure Aryan Germans could wear the the clothing of murdered Jews. The Germans did the same thing with the clothes taken from Jews in other concentration camps, while Hitler spent his nation's resources on armaments. There were no barracks in Bełżec; there was no work for the prisoners, they were gassed upon arrival. The Nazis were in a hurry.

After our "visit," Sarah took us to "her" school, where a simple meal of gruel soup and fried fish were served to us and to the students. We

---

18   In Bełżec extermination camp, 434,508 were murdered over the course of nine months, from March to December 1942.

met a small group of children who'd finished their lunch and were singing Hebrew prayers. Many were Russian, enjoying summer camp at the end of their school year. These children had a difficult life at home, some with only one parent, some orphans. In Sarah's school, they were able to eat one nourishing meal a day, study general subjects, as well as Hebrew and religion. They learned how to cultivate a garden, to grow flowers, berries, and fruit trees. The cooks, teachers, and other employees were all Ukrainian; Sarah was the only Jew. There were very few Jews in Lwów to perform such jobs.

We met Sarah's husband, Rabbi Bald, before his evening service. When we asked him about a reform synagogue in Lwów, he had no knowledge of any. We told him that our Temple Israel in Long Beach, California, had presented a Torah to the rabbi who served the reformed synagogue in Lwów. To Rabbi Bald, the only synagogue was his conservative synagogue. When I pressed him on the subject, he suddenly remembered the name of another rabbi, guessing that our Torah must have gone to Kiev. Unfortunately, I had forgotten to bring Rabbi Duckovny's card, still on my refrigerator door at home in Long Beach. It had been quite a while since Rabbi Duckovny had taken the Torah back with him to Europe, and it was possible that he traveled between cities, performing religious services in each large Ukrainian city. In any case, he was not located in Lwów. But it was puzzling that Rabbi Bald did not want to acknowledge the existence of the reform rabbi until we pressed him with more questions. As far as he was concerned, the reform synagogue and the reform rabbi were a closed subject.

We visited the area that had been the Lwów ghetto. Like other parts of the city, the former ghetto had been seriously neglected—potholes in the roads, broken stairs and windows, and dilapidated walls in need of repair. Harold and I happened to notice holes on the right side of the front door that once held a *mezuzah* (doorpost in Hebrew), containing verses from Deuteronomy. A woman who lived in one of the homes told us that the holes had been repaired several times but nothing had stuck—no putty or sealant stayed fixed in the holes. It was as if some power were keeping the holes open to remind the present-day occupiers of the house that Jews had lived there before them—Jews who'd been ousted and murdered by the Nazis.

Early the next morning, we left Lwów to catch a plane for Israel. We had trouble crossing the border due to a long line of semis and cars, stretching for miles. Several lanes of cars waited to cross the checkpoint. Traffic was at a standstill. The day grew hotter and more humid with each passing minute, and Bolek lamented that we'd be stuck there until nightfall. He got out of the car to assess the situation. As he was coming back to the car, a small car drove from the opposite direction, stopping next to us. Two men got out of their car and Bolek spoke to them briefly, then he got into the back seat as one of the Ukrainian men slipped into the driver's seat, driving very fast to the checkpoint booth. He spoke on the phone to border guards, telling them that he was bringing us. When we got there, he jumped out of the car and was gone. Bolek returned to the driver's seat and smiled as we crossed the border. After we were safely on the Polish side, he told us that the two men were Ukrainian mafia who worked with the border police—that was how they made extra money. Because our car had Polish registration plates, they felt that they could talk business with us. This quickie cost us $50 and was worth every penny. The next morning, Bolek drove us to the Kraków airport and without any problems, we left for Israel.

It was our ninth or tenth trip to Israel. In 1962, on our first trip there, we had been the young leadership representatives of the Long Beach Jewish Community and the only couple from the West Coast. We met Ben Gurion, Golda Meir, young Shimon Peres, and other Israeli luminaries. We saw our friends and distant relatives. We wanted them to know that we thought of them, that we supported them, and to tell them that they were not alone in their new country, surrounded by enemies. We were very proud of this new tiny Jewish country.

We spent six wonderful days in Israel, going to Jerusalem for a day to see all the new construction around the city. We managed to see a new exhibit of a computerized model of the Temple before its destruction. We even squeezed in a dinner at *Abugosh*, a restaurant in an Arab village in a suburb of Jerusalem, where they served the best St. Peter's fish.

We visited an antiques dealer who sold me a pair of Viennese candleholders, dating back to the early 18th century. They were as tall but less ornate than our old ones, appropriated by the Soviets in 1940 in Przemśyl.

Our next destination was England to visit relatives and friends. While there, we helped my cousin, Fred Marshall Mantel, celebrate his 80th birthday, and we visited a distant cousin, Bertek Gottlieb, in Nottingham. Then we checked into a hotel in London, turned in our rental car, and used roomy London taxis to get around the city. Four days was not much time to spend in that glorious city, but if one cannot walk very well and had to depend on taxis only, London got very pricey. Of course, we visited the Gottliebs and Ludek, and Harold got on famously. As always, it was great to return home and appreciate once again the freedom and beauty of California.

FREEDOM WRITERS

Some people have read *The Freedom Writers Diary: How a Teacher and 150 Teens Used Writing to Change Themselves and the World Around Them*, written by Erin Gruwell and her students. Many others have seen the film, *Freedom Writers*, based on the book and starring Hilary Swank. Although I didn't appear in the movie, I was mentioned in the book several times and played a part in that four-year project at Wilson High School in Long Beach, where Erin taught.

Wilson High School also happened to be the school that my three children attended. I gave lectures there to students studying European history, World War II, and the Holocaust.[19]

Erin was a young teacher on her first assignment and had been given a class of very difficult ninth graders at Wilson. They were of mixed ethnic and national backgrounds, kids from the "hood," kids who had seen drive-by shootings, who dealt drugs, who had been abused by parents or relatives—tough kids who didn't think that studying was cool and who had no plans to graduate. Erin entered the classroom for the first time wearing a simple navy dress with a pearl necklace, took one look at those kids and said to herself that she wouldn't last more than a week at her job. The students took one look at her and thought the same thing.

---

19   For many years I have lectured at different high schools about my wartime experiences.

But something unusual happened during the first few weeks of school. There was one student who was particularly difficult to manage. One day, Erin found a caricature of that boy's face floating among giggling students. Erin got angry and wanted to find out who'd done the drawing. She told the students that she wouldn't tolerate such prejudice and that the cruel caricature reminded her of anti-Semitic cartoons that had been widely circulated in Europe before the Holocaust. But her students had never heard of the Holocaust, which is why she decided to invite Mr. Mermelstine to her class, a survivor of Auschwitz, who happened to be my neighbor. I had read about Erin inviting Mr. Mermelstine in the *Long Beach Press Telegram* and called Erin to congratulate her on asking a Holocaust survivor to speak to her class. She then invited me to speak to her class on March 26, 1996. I developed a great kinship with these tough kids. They called me "grandma," and we seemed to understand each other. They were very touched by my story.

I attended the end-of-year picnic, where each and every student got up and spoke about their problems and how "Ms. G" had helped them to cope. They had developed love and respect for her, because she had made them believe in themselves. There wasn't a dry eye at that picnic, and there was no more talk of students dropping out of school.

The students spent many hours after school, staying with Erin to work on extra projects, sometimes leaving the classroom through the window because the school was shut down for the night. Luckily, their room was on the ground floor.

Thanks to the philanthropy of billionaire entrepreneur, John Tu of Kingston Technology,[20] Erin's whole class would fly to Washington D.C. for Memorial Day weekend. I was invited as a chaperone, and Harold was invited as class doctor. An entire United Airlines jet was booked just for us. Most of the kids had never been on an airplane; most of them had never been out of Long Beach. The excitement was high, but they all had

---

20   John Tu credits his success to the unique opportunity that America offers immigrants like himself to achieve their dreams. He said, "I can tell you that I feel the founding fathers of American had the right idea: immigration has made this rich culture, this great environment of what is often called the melting pot."

to promise to behave: no smoking, no drinking, no drugs or else they'd be sent home, and their parents would have to pay for their tickets.

There were no behavioral problems among the students during our four-day trip. We stayed at the big, luxurious Marriot Hotel, and the kids were thrilled with their accommodations, never having stayed at a hotel before, let alone one so elegant. They all behaved like ladies and gentlemen. We visited Arlington cemetery and JFK's grave. We went to several museums, including the Holocaust museum. We visited the White House and heard interesting speakers. On the last night, holding hands, 150 strong, we walked through the streets of Washington, stopping traffic all the way to the Washington Monument, where we lit candles and sang.

It was a once-in-a-lifetime experience for the students and for us adults, as well.

Later on in the year, a young girl from Bosnia, Zlata Filipovic, came to visit Erin's class for a week in May. Zlata, fifteen years old—the same age as the students at Wilson—had written her own diary about living in war-torn Bosnia. She and her family had been lucky to leave Bosnia, moving to Ireland, where she was able to continue to write. Her book was compared to *The Diary of Anne Frank*. Zlata had a lot in common with the students and enjoyed attending their classes and socializing with them. They showed her the sights of Long Beach. I stayed in touch with Zlata. We exchanged Christmas cards, and a few years ago, she contacted me because she'd written another book and was scheduled to talk about it at the Skirball Museum. Harold and I spent an evening together with her, reminiscing about the past.

Another guest who visited the Wilson High students was none other than the brave Miep Gies, who, along with her husband and two others, was instrumental in hiding Anne Frank's family. I participated in those activities and enjoyed them as much as the students did. At that time the students were involved in writing their diaries. They were told to write whatever touched them deeply, both in school and in their lives. They struggled at times with their problems, families, friends, and life. It was hard for some of them to admit that people were mean to them. Many felt their problems were insurmountable and that giving up would be far easier than struggling. But they didn't give up. In their senior year, they collectively won a coveted Anne Frank Award, traditionally awarded to a single person. Fifty of the students flew to New York to accept the award. Again, I was invited to fly along with the group.

While we were in New York, Erin Gruwell talked to publishers regarding the diary. The students were interviewed on ABC TV. They attended the Broadway production of *Anne Frank*, starring Natalie Portman.

Nearly all the students graduated from Wilson High School, and most of them enrolled in colleges. Some were the first in their families to hold a high school diploma. In the eyes of their families, they had achieved greatness. One of the Freedom Writers became a teacher herself, and I gave lectures in her class two years in a row.

Erin turned around the lives of 150 students 360 degrees. It was truly a success story, and I was so glad to have been part of it. In Erin's book are photographs of the time we held a basketball game at Long Beach State University to raise funds for Bosnia. There are photos of me, John Tu, and others. Several teams were named after Anne Frank, Zlata Filipovic, John Tu, and, I'm proud to say, myself. I still have the jersey with my name on it.

Erin invited us to the film screening of *Freedom Writers*. The students, Erin, and the parents felt very proud to have been involved in the project. The movie was quite good, but Hollywood changed the story to enhance the drama. There was less actual violence at Wilson than portrayed in the film. Erin was well portrayed by Hilary Swank.

BEŁŻEC MEMORIAL

The first time Harold and I visited Bełżec, it was a huge, empty and neglected field that had a broken wooden stand and a few bricks on the ground on which were written words of remembrance. I picked up some rusted barbed wire and leaves that had fallen from trees and took them home as the only memento of that dreadful place.

For years, I couldn't bring myself to talk or even think about how my Mamusia and Richard were rounded up. Was she petrified or was she calm, trying to pacify my eleven-year-old cousin? Was she hopeful that somehow she and Richard would survive? Did my mother hold Richard's hand as they walked down that dreadful corridor, naked and freezing, prodded by vicious guards to the gas chamber? What were her final thoughts? Was she resigned to her fate? I'll never know the answers to these questions. I never had a chance to say a proper goodbye, to kiss her or feel her embrace once more. And I can't begin to imagine my father's pain in parting with his wife and watching as the barbaric SS shouted at her and cousin Richard, marching them away for transport. Did he have a moment to say goodbye?

In 2005, we again visited the Bełżec Memorial Site, which by then had become a true memorial to many thousands of victims, my mother and cousin among them. Maybe by visiting the memorial, I was able to see the place where their lives had come to an end, the awful place I still see in my dreams.

We went to Bełżec in late afternoon. The place was eerie and desolate. The train tracks where Jews once got off the Nazi cattle cars were now engraved with Stars of David. The autumn wind rustled the leaves, and if you listened carefully, you could almost hear the cries of the 500,000 Jews and thousands of Gypsies who were put to death in the gas chambers, using carbon monoxide. In the distance was a huge field covered with dark crushed stones that serve as grave markers.

A young guard told us that the memorial would be closing in fifteen minutes and that we should come back the next day. I told him I was a Holocaust survivor and that my mother had ended up in this camp, adding that I was unable to come the following day. The guard then called his boss and after a brief consultation, we were told we could go in and stay as long as we wanted and that we didn't have to pay the entrance fees. Hebrew letters drip rust down a wall, saying, "Never forget." We asked the guard why the letters were rusting only two years after the memorial had been installed. He answered that it had been done on purpose, to seem as if tears were running down the wall. We walked on a road called Crevasse that grew higher and narrower as we neared the top of the walk. Thousands upon thousands of first names are etched into granite walls on both sides. On one side is a quotation from the Book of Job 16:18: "Earth, do not cover my blood. Let there be no resting place for my outcry."

What I keep, though, is a vivid memory of that wonderful lady who was not only my mother but also the best friend I've ever had. Visiting the magnificent memorial again gave me a sense that there was a final resting place for her and all the victims of Bełżec.

In 2001, Harold and I dedicated a beautiful outdoor memorial at the Long Beach Jewish Community Center in honor of my parents, Henryk and Edyta Krebs, who perished at the hands of the Nazis. Our daughter, Julia, wrote the following poem, incised in concrete:

In an old wooden frame, the backing coming out,

Stands a photograph.

Old, yellowing, cracked with age, faded.

A woman's face can be clearly seen.

A stranger to my eyes, yet I've always known her name.

A smile like that of my own,

Her gentle brown eyes

Expressing the warmth I never felt.

I see our two lives connecting as one.

Grandmother, our lives may have been separated

By more than a war,

But through this old photograph you live again.

THE HIDDEN CHILD

In June 2006, several unexpected things happened. I had submitted my Lwów article to Rachelle Goldstein, editor of *The Hidden Child* newsletter the year before. Rachelle had assured me that she'd publish it when the next letter came out. I had completely forgotten about it, until one day I received a fat brown envelope in the mail. Upon opening it, I found about a dozen copies of the newsletter containing my article entitled "Return to Lwów."

I was so pleased to see my article in print, even though it took almost three years after I had written it. A short time later, I received an email from Rachelle, asking if she could give my email address to a woman in San Francisco who had read my article. I said yes, and the next day the woman called. She was a dentist who was calling during office hours and sounded nervous because she was leaving for Poland in three days and had made no hotel reservations. She needed a name of a driver to Lwów. I gave her all the necessary information. During our short conversation, I learned that before coming to America, she had left Poland and gone to England. I asked her when that had been, and she replied that she'd traveled by ship in March of 1946 on a transport of war orphans, led by Rabbi Schonfeld! I told her that I'd sailed on the same ship but hadn't met her or other fellow travelers, because I'd been seasick for most of the trip. I knew that I'd hear from her when she returned from Poland.

The next day, I received another email from a woman called Halinka. She had come from Lwów and had lived in Manhattan, but moved to Florida after her husband's death. She had no children. She was eager to talk to me and we seemed to have a lot in common. I asked her how she'd come to the United States, and she too had been on the same transport of orphans as mine to England—another coincidence! Because of my one published article in *The Hidden Child*, I connected with many people after sixty years. I never thought it would bring so many new acquaintances. As we talked, I found out that Halinka had gone to school in Lwów, so I asked if, by any chance, she had known Anita Seltzer. She became very excited, telling me that she and Anita had been the best of friends in school. She didn't know that Anita had survived and was ready to call her at once.

I had met Anita, a lovely and gentle lady, in Katowice in 1946. She and her mother had survived the war and still lived in Katowice. After I left Poland, Anita and her mother also left Poland, moving to Paris. For a while, we kept in touch, but after a few years we stopped writing for some reason. I found Anita again through her relatives in San Francisco, who gave me her address in Australia, where she taught English and French in high school. From then on, we continued a warm friendship; Harold and I visited them in Melbourne and they came to visit us in Long Beach. Anita's son and daughter visited us as well, and our son, Philip, saw them in Melbourne while taking an extra course for medical school at Tufts. In 2015 her letters stopped coming. After a long period of not getting answers to my letters, I wrote to her son. He promised to deliver my messages. Eventually, he told me that she was losing her memory. In 2017, he wrote to tell me of her passing. I had lost an old and very good friend.

During my conversation with Halinka, I brought up another name, Halina Aleksander. I couldn't remember Halina's maiden name, but I mentioned Korner, the surname of her grandparents. She said she knew a Halinka Lemel, another best friend. "Yes, Yes!" I shouted, "That's the same Halinka! Lemel was her maiden name."

We were both astounded that within thirty minutes, two total strangers had found so many people in common. Halinka sang the three songs we'd learned on the ship en route to England: "Daisy," "You Are My Sunshine," and "It Ain't Gonna Rain No More" and we reminisced about the wonderful Rabbi Schonfeld.[21] After we talked, I dialed Halina Aleksander's house in Kraków, Poland, and told her about the other Halina in Florida. She was so happy to hear this news. All of a sudden I had connected three women who had known each other over 60 years ago, and I found two women who shared the same experiences, leaving Poland in 1946, sailing to Britain on the very same Swedish ship as I had.

---

21   In 1962 Harold and I had the chance to visit Rabbi Schonfeld at his school in London
     for girls and boys. He saved the lives of more than 4,000 children in Kindertransports
     during the war. When he died at the age of 72 in 1984, his obituary appeared in both the
     Los Angeles Times and the *Long Beach Press Telegram*. It was reported that 2,000 people
     followed his funeral cortege in the north of London.

TRIP TO ISRAEL AND POLAND

Harold and I went to Israel for a week in 2006 to visit relatives and friends. It must've been our eighth or ninth visit to Israel. Afterward, we flew to Warsaw where we spent a day with our friend, Eva Kujawa. I wanted to meet Irena Sendler, a wonderful brave lady who was ninety-six years old at the time. When she was in her early twenties, she'd smuggled 2,500 Jewish children out of the Warsaw Ghetto, placed them with Christian families in convents, orphanages, and churches. She wrote the children's names, birthdates, and parents' names on tissue paper and stuffed them into a jar, later burying it in someone's yard under a tree. After the war, the children who had survived would know their beginnings and might be reunited with any surviving family members. Irena had been caught by the Nazis, was tortured and sentenced to die, but at the last minute, the Polish underground bribed a Nazi and saved her life.

The children Irena had saved were now caring for her. As her health was fragile, I was told that it might not be possible for me to meet this courageous human being. Irena had saved her caregiver, Elżbieta, when she was only six months old. Elżbieta never saw her birth parents, but her adoptive mother had been very good to her. At the time I called her, Elżbieta was grieving the loss of her husband, who had died six weeks earlier. A friend from Montréal was staying with her to keep her company. When she told me the name of her friend, Renata Saidman, I said that I had met her at meetings for Hidden Children in Denver, Colorado. What a small world it was! I had planned to meet Renata in Warsaw. Renata had been another of the many children saved by Irena Sendler.

MOTHER'S BUILDING
IN PRZEMYŚL

During the Solidarity movement in Poland, led by Lech Wałęsa, workers raised their voices in protest and went on strike against unfair labor practices. The movement eventually prevailed in pushing communist Poland toward more democratic reforms. In 1989 there were, for the first time, free elections in one of the Communist bloc countries, and Poland became the first non-Communist government in the Soviet bloc. (Six months later, the Berlin Wall fell.)

After upheavals in Poland, we traveled back there several times, hiring a lawyer in Przemyśl concerning my mother's building. I was asked to produce the death certificates of my parents, which, of course, I did not have because the Nazis had murdered them, leaving no records. The procedure we had to follow was to place an ad in the newspaper. If my parents were still alive, they might read the newspaper notice and claim ownership of their building. These newspaper ads had to remain in the newspaper for six months.

After several trips, and after filling out many legal forms, I was asked to appear in the Przemyśl City Court for a judgment. In the courtroom, I had to stand in a fenced-in area, like in an English court, and give answers to the judge's questions. Finally, she gave her decision: I, in fact, was the legal and rightful owner of my mother's building where I'd spent my childhood years. Reclaiming ownership of the building gave me great satisfaction and pride in my family heritage. Because the majority of Jews in Poland had been murdered at the hands of the Nazis, few survivors were left to claim their homes, buildings, or lands.

Finally, in 2008, I managed to sell the house to the manager of the building. I discovered that there were plans to add another story to the house where the attic used to be. If I had more time ahead of me, I might have waited longer before selling, because I had a feeling that real estate values would increase in that area. But I sold the house when I had a chance; it was easier than having my children deal with a complicated transaction in Polish, a language they didn't speak.

I doubt that I'll return to Przemyśl again, and it makes me sad that my connection with the city of my birth has ended. Yet walking on Przemyśl streets, seeing old familiar buildings of my childhood made me feel vulnerable, as if I were a young child again. No matter what experiences you have as an adult, you always treasure memories of your hometown and growing up.

THE DIARY OF ANNE FRANK OPERA

The Long Beach Opera sent a condensed version of *The Diary of Anne Frank* opera into schools in 2007-2015, introducing students not only to the opera but also to me, an actual Holocaust survivor. After each performance, I went onstage and told my own story.

Each year, there were about six to ten performances at different high and junior high schools. The eighth, ninth, and tenth grade students were very receptive to the half-hour show, presenting one opera singer and a pianist. Most students had never heard an opera before, and although the music was quite modern, they seemed to enjoy it.

After the performance, I went onstage to talk to the students for a full hour. After my talk, there was a question-and-answer period. They were often too shy to ask anything at first, but later, when the students gathered around me, they asked plenty of questions, took pictures with me, shook my hand and hugged me. They felt more comfortable when we spoke directly to one other. It was a wonderful experience both for the students and me. Though funding for the opera ran out in 2015, I am gratified to learn that the opera will once again be presented in the schools.

As time goes on, World War II and the Nazi atrocities get farther and farther removed from the younger generations' knowledge. Very few survivors remain alive and hopefully, I will be able to speak to the students once again. Such an experience has been shown to make a greater emotional impact on students than reading about the Holocaust in textbooks. Many of the students, after hearing me tell my story, promise to "never forget."

YOM HASHOAH

At the beginning of the 21st century, I revived the annual commemoration of Yom Hashoah, Holocaust Remembrance Day, at the Long Beach Jewish Community Center. I chaired that event for the next twelve years, because it was important to remember the terrible deeds perpetrated against the Jewish people during the war.

Each year, we got the whole community involved in the commemoration. Usually we had a rabbi represent the religious community, and survivors would light six memorial candles, each candle representing one million of the six million who were murdered. We tried to involve school-aged children to write essays, poems and music, and we invited a guest speaker.

One year, we invited Clifford Michaels from Tulsa, Oklahoma, who was a twenty-one-year-old soldier who'd liberated a concentration camp in 1945. I invited him to participate and to read aloud the letter he'd written to his family from Europe. He accepted the invitation and asked if he could visit the Queen Mary while he was in Long Beach—the ship on which he'd sailed to Europe during the war.

April 18, 1945

Dear Folks,

Have just returned from a newly liberated German concentration camp. It is less than a week since we got here. I would like to tell you what I saw. It is a large camp (50,000 men) but considered small in comparison to other camps. It is located on a high hill, near a rock quarry. There is a wonderful view, but I don't think prisoners had much time to admire the view.

The camp housed 50,000, but disease, starvation and murder reduced the numbers to 20,000 inside the last six weeks. Others were dying of starvation even as we were looking the camp over. Food was available but not until tomorrow will it be comparable in quality and quantity to the food that we eat.

The guide said most happily, "Tomorrow, if we get the same food as you get, it will be excellent!" He said he had examined our rations and found them excellent. It really made us ashamed of our complaints about eating out of cans. He said that he had a little soup, bread and margarine and was forced to work on this diet all day long.

The prisoners worked very hard until they dropped dead. Some prisoners were hung by their arms (behind their backs) in the camp and then taken to a nearby forest and shot. Our guide told us, that there were still bodies in the forest who had been machine gunned and never buried. I suppose the Germans had no time for it before we arrived.

We saw the crematory and could see charred skeletons quite plainly. 20,000 bodies could be burned in a day and the furnaces had gone full blast for a day and a half. Saw a room full of naked dead bodies of prisoners, who died of malnutrition in the previous day or two. There were shelves on each side and they slept side by side, packed in like Sardines. The

*bunks were stacked four high and the bedclothes were lousy.
American ambulances were making trip after trip to the camp,
to take the worst cases to where they could get medical attention. Those who could walk, wandered aimlessly around, others were lying on the bed and asked us for cigarettes, candy,
and sugar. There was a group of German civilians in their
best clothes, taking a forced tour of the camp. Our guide told
us, that the German women cried and said: Hitler had lied
to them. The guide told us that there were German political
prisoners who were allowed to have visitors. Also, the camp
prisoners cleaned up bomb damage in the nearby towns. So
the German people knew what the score was or just deliber-
ately closed their eyes.*

*Well enough about this subject. If you have an opportunity to
see movies or snapshots of these places, be sure and see them.
I don't believe you need to worry about us. GIs are not being
too easy on the Germans.*

All my love,

Clifford Michaels Jr.

The 60th Anniversary of the liberation of Auschwitz occurred on
May 2005, the same day that I chaired the Yom Hashoah at the Long Beach
Jewish Community Center. The attendance was better than we expected,
and Newmans Green's presentation was excellent. I had wanted to participate in the ceremonies in Kraków, but the more I thought about it, the more
the trip seemed impossible. I could never have traveled on buses with my
power chair or even with my old walker.[22] By 2005, I was also using a
motorized scooter outside. Getting up and down on buses and walking
in grass or mud was out of the question. As it turned out, the weather in
Poland was cold and wet, so those who were there complained bitterly.

---

22   For ten years prior to 2005, I was forced to use a walker in order to get anywhere. My
     physical condition was neuropathy, arthritis, and spinal surgeries that caused debilitating
     damage and progressive disabilities.

Ron Frydman, a member of ADL and Jackie Luk from the L.A. office had attended the event in Poland and later showed us slides of the trip. As Ron commented on them, I realized that he couldn't see the slides the way a survivor could see them. Nor could he quite understand what living under Nazis or being an inmate at a camp was like.

At times I think I have imagined certain experiences and occurrences during the war, and no sooner do I doubt they happened, when I read in a book or an article about a Holocaust survivor who had exactly the same feelings, thoughts, or experiences; and then it makes me feel validated.

Sometimes I wonder why I still read other people's Holocaust memoirs. Perhaps I was meant to live and tell the story of the Holocaust, which I have been doing for more than forty years. Yet I still have a constant need to know more and more about the Holocaust.

Is it because I didn't suffer enough? I didn't starve like those who were in the camps. I wasn't beaten and I had a roof over my head, but I still suffered by being alone with no one to share my feelings with. I suffered because I couldn't grieve for my mother, my dearest Mamusia. I suffered because I never knew who might report me to the police. I suffered because of the constant fear of being discovered, that one of the Tarasiuk children may say a wrong word to a wrong person and the Gestapo would arrive at our door and kill us.

I suffered because I lived a lie.

I suffered because I'd lost my dearest, brave father, whom I'd hoped to see again when the war ended.

In *Together* magazine, I read an article on the anniversary events held in Auschwitz about the many dignitaries who attended and what they all had to say. Despite their well-intentioned words, anti-Semitism is alive and well in Russia, Poland, Germany, France, England, Belgium, Sweden, and the United States. Anti-Semitism doesn't have a country or borders. It may have changed its shape and symbols and rallying cries; it may be different from the far-right anti-Semitism of the Third Reich, but it lurks today in many countries and in many different forms. That is why it is important to fight against anti-Semitism. Pope Francis, who in 2016 visited Auschwitz, made an address to the International Conference in 2018. He began by saying that "indifference is a virus that is dangerously contagious in our time." He went on, "In order to recover our humanity, to recover our human understanding of reality and to overcome so many deplorable forms of apathy towards our neighbor, we need this memory, this capacity to involve ourselves together in remembering. Memory is the key to accessing the future, and it is our responsibility to hand it on in a dignified way to young generations."

That is why, each year, it is so vitally important to commemorate the Shoah, to never ever forget.

MY HEART IS A VIOLIN

I received a book in the mail, *My Heart is a Violin,* by Shony Alex Braun, a great talent. Braun's bright future as a violinist was cut short by the Nazis who deported him and his family to Auschwitz. Later, in the death camp of Dachau, he miraculously survived because of a violin. In 1994, his "Symphony of the Holocaust" for violin and orchestra, was nominated for a Pulitzer Prize. He died from Alzheimer's in 1992, but I was fortunate enough to meet him on two occasions when he played violin at parties, classical as well as Yiddish and Hungarian tunes. He played with such gusto and feeling, it made one feel like singing and dancing. I have some of his tapes and each time I hear them, I think of my childhood, and the music brings back warm memories.

In June 2003, I visited the Museum of Tolerance in Los Angeles to view an exhibit of Freidl Dicker-Brandeis, who had studied in the Bauhaus, a German art school, and was a well-known artist before the war. She and her husband were imprisoned in Theresienstadt concentration camp in 1942, where she taught children to draw. Somehow, in the optimistic atmosphere she created, the children were able to forget about hunger and being separated from their parents who had probably already been killed. The Nazis "beautified" Theresienstadt in 1943 for an inspection by the

Swiss Red Cross. The following year, Dicker-Brandeis was transported to Auschwitz, where she perished, together with many innocent children.

It is impossible to guess the immense loss of future geniuses who perished in the Holocaust: poets and writers, painters and composers, philosophers and historians, mathematicians and doctors, social activists and politicians, lawyers and jurists, inventors and entrepreneurs, skiers and swimmers, chess players and soccer players, generals and soldiers, teachers and students, parents and children.

SINCE THEN

I have given several oral histories to organizations, The USC Shoah Foundation, The Holocaust Museum in Washington D.C., The Los Angeles Holocaust Museum and others. In those speaking engagements, I wasn't able to give details about my relatives because of the limited time frame. Since most of them perished in the Holocaust, I feel it proper and necessary that their stories should be recorded in this document. Both my parents' families came from Przemyśl. The book of records goes only as far back as my grandparents.

On my father's side was his father, Pesach Krebs, who married Gitla Kleiner, from Tarnow, Poland. They had two children: Evelina and Henryk, my father, born on January 7, 1891.

My grandfather's wife, Gitla, died at a young age. I saw her photo in my father's watch. She was a very beautiful woman. My grandfather remarried. His second wife, Genia, whom I remember well, used to come to the store and sit at the little desk, trying to help with customers. I don't know how much she really helped, but she felt good assisting in the store. She had silver grey hair, always kissed me and hugged me, and was a very quiet and lovely lady. She died of old age during the war.

My aunt, Evelina or Eva, married Molek Mantel and they moved to Vienna. Later, they moved to Munich, which they left for England in 1938. They had to learn English, a rather difficult task for older people. Uncle

Mantel was lucky to obtain a job as a filing clerk in a store. Many men in the same situation aged quickly and never accepted their new lifestyle; many committed suicide. When the Germans started bombing London, the Mantels moved north to Yorkshire and settled in Leeds, where I went in March 1946. Aunt Eva spoke fluent Polish and German and was able to learn the rudiments of English so that she could shop for groceries. She wasn't comfortable conversing with English people.

My grandfather, Pesach Krebs, and his second wife had one child, Berta. She married Leon Oberhardt, a lawyer, and they had two daughters, Irena and Lidia. Both cousins were slightly older than I was and lived in Przemyśl. The whole family perished—most likely in one of the concentration camps.

My mother came from a much larger family. There were seven children: four sisters, and three brothers.

Grandfather David Goliger was born in 1860, married Chaja, Rivka (Regina) Rubinfeld, who came from Zalesie, near Krasiczyn, villages close to Przemyśl.

The oldest daughter, Mina Goliger, married young. Her husband, Mondschein, whose first name I forget, was the head of the railroad station in Stryj—an unusual position of importance for a Jew in those days. They had one daughter, Dora, who received a Ph.D. in philosophy. Dora married Dr. Korn and they lived in Katowice. They had no children.

Samuel Goliger, an engineer, owned a large apartment building in Przemyśl. He married Helena, and they had two daughters, Irena and Lila. The entire family did not survive; likely they perished in Auschwitz.

Zofia, an accomplished pianist, married a physician, Wilhelm Schwarzer, and they lived in Jarosław, a half-hour ride by train from Przemyśl. Before she married, Zofia played piano with concert orchestras. Her husband played violin, and often they played duets together for their own enjoyment. Wilhelm had a busy general practice, and aunt Zofia was his assistant. They had two children, Zygmunt and Danuta. Danusia, as we called her, was a year or two older than I. She developed pernicious anemia when she was about seven years old, for which there was no cure. Her parents traveled with her to the best doctors in Vienna to obtain the best medical care, but she died at the age of eight. Aunt Zofia was never herself after she lost her Danusia and never played the piano again. The whole family, except for Zygmunt, perished. Zofia and Wilhelm were hiding in my uncle's building, together with Zygmunt's girlfriend, Renia Spiegel. A neighbor must have reported them to the Gestapo. They were led to the street and shot there. Adolf Goliger escaped Poland through Romania. He went to Israel. He married but had no children, dying in 1960. I don't know what happened to his wife.

Henryk, the youngest brother, survived the war but died in 1950 of heart disease.

Zygmunt survived Bergen-Belsen and Auschwitz. He immigrated to the United States, and practiced pediatrics in New York. In 1955 he was drafted into the Air Force and was stationed in San Bernardino, California. He and his wife subsequently had two children, Mitchell and Pamela. Zygmunt died in 2004 from an illness caused by his physical experiences in the concentration camps.

My distant cousins, the Schochets, related to the Krebs family, were sent deep into Russia. They survived the war and have lived in Israel since before 1948.

Millie and Vincent Benn, my very close friends in England, died at the ripe old ages of 96 and 97. Their daughter, Julia, married and had one daughter, Elizabeth. Her brother, Nicholas, became a doctor, husband, and had two children. Julia sent me some drawings that I made for her in honor of her seventh birthday in 1946 when I lived with her family in Otley. The drawings show a couple dressed in a Polish national costume. I never expected Julia to save them, but it was a wonderful gift to remind me of my early days with her family in England.[23]

---

23 Liz liked these drawings well enough to ask for them. She framed them and they decorate her walls, though I never thought them worthy of being displayed. I feel a bit like Grandma Moses!

EPILOGUE

In 2018, I had my 91st birthday. I lost seventy pounds over a year and a half, though I didn't diet. Somehow, I lost my sense of taste, my sense of smell, and my appetite, and voilà—the weight melted away. It's true that I can't walk anymore and I lose my balance and fall frequently. I've lost power in my arms and hands and I have trouble combing my hair and brushing my teeth. But I'm still here.

Harold recently closed his practice after fifty-one years. My grandchildren are all teenagers. Madison is in college, Eli had his Bar Mitzvah and will enter college next year, and Chelsea has begun eleventh grade. The preschool that Lois and I began in the 1970s at Alpert Jewish Community Center is now considered the finest nursery school in Long Beach with a long waiting list of new applicants. Its roster of students is diverse—children of different nationalities, religions, and ethnicities. Each time I enter the Jewish Center, I see happy children running, skipping, and laughing along the corridor, and their parents or grandparents picking them from school. They all seem safe in that environment. I think of the early beginnings of the preschool, and my heart swells with pride.

Sitting in our family room and facing the back wall of our backyard garden, covered with white and red climbing roses, I'm writing the final sentences of my memoir. Nasturtiums have grown in the corner in their velvety orange and yellow colors, and the sun is shining brightly. Delicate pale pink lilies grace the coffee table, so how bad can it be? But I am still in my own house where I enjoy my garden and the beautiful California weather. Harold and I have each other, and we continue to live in our home that we built in 1965. We are still of clear mind and enjoy music, friends, and freedom—reasons to be thankful for.

I am so grateful that my children have grown to be great human beings, smart, decent, and loving. Their children are also shaping up to make us proud and even their dogs are lovely pets, pleasant to be with.

Fewer and fewer Holocaust survivors are still living, and so as long as I have the opportunity, I will share my testimony of how hatred led to the worst genocide in history. Standing up and speaking out might make listeners better understand the horrors of the past and wish not to repeat them. That is my fervent wish. My one regret is that I will never have enough time to read all the books on my shelves.

Gerda Krebs Seifer
December 2018
Long Beach, California

AFTERWORD

Next to being a Holocaust survivor oneself, marriage to a survivor is the closest one could be to experiencing this horrible event. I am sure not a day goes by without Gerda thinking of her dear mother and devoted father who were victims. Gerda has spent years giving presentations of her story before students in public and private schools, in universities, and at a number of institutions. Together, we installed a memorial to her parents in an alcove at the Jewish Community Center of Long Beach. But the culmination of her work is publishing this memoir. In ten or fifteen years, there will be no living survivor, but her story can be read and should be read by the next generations to remind them: "Never Forget."

—Harold Seifer, M.D.
November 7, 2018
Long Beach, California

AFTERWORD

When my Mom, my Mamusia, told me she was going to write this book, I never doubted she would accomplish what many would have considered a daunting, if not impossible, goal. But my Mamusia has never let fear hold her back. She has had so many incredibly difficult challenges in life, and she's faced them all with intelligence, determination, and strength. I asked her how she was able to survive the unbelievable pain of losing her parents, her relatives, and the seemingly insurmountable challenges of starting her life over in a world so foreign to her, and her answer was simply "because I had to, I had no other choice." But she didn't just survive; she built a life for herself and has inspired many along the way.

I was in high school when I discovered a rare picture of my mother's mother, my grandmother, and I instantly felt a surge of grief and sadness, knowing I would never meet her, never get to feel her warm hug or see her beautiful smile. I would never get to meet my grandfather or look into his bright blue eyes. But through my mother's stories, I felt a sense of connection, and while it's hard to describe, I also felt a sense of pride and love. She told me that her parents were strong, beautiful, smart and loving--so loving and so determined, they did everything in their power to protect their daughter, so that she could live to be able to tell their story.

This is their story, but it is also many other people's stories of survival, perseverance, coming face to face with indescribable evil, but also of fierce courage and love. I'm so proud of my Mamusia and so proud to be her daughter, and the granddaughter of Edyta and Henryk Krebs. And I am thrilled that her story--and their stories--will be read by generations to come. Never again. Never forget.

Julia Seifer
February 26, 2019
Pasadena, CA

AFTERWORD

On her motorized scooter, Gerda opened the door with her head cocked slightly to one side, her light, clear eyes taking my measure. It was our first meeting. She invited me inside, showing me boxes and envelopes overflowing with pages she'd written over decades about her experiences in Poland during the Holocaust. She told me her story. She showed me many prized possessions, collected from around the world: paintings, pottery, glass, and most especially, the green plants of her garden. There was a certain reassurance in our tour, that despite all whom she has lost and all she has endured, beauty remains a sustaining force in her life and *things grow*.

At the end of the interview about whether or not I would help her assemble all her notes and pages into a memoir, I told Gerda to take time in thinking over whether she'd like to work with me. "I don't have to think it over," she said, pointing a long, green-lacquered fingernail at me. "I *know*," she said, "I know right away when I like somebody."

It is that trust that has guided us through the past year, trust that has matured and grown round, like the ripe figs she made me pluck from the bushes in her yard. "Not that one, *that* one!" she would demand, making me reach ever higher, dodging a squadron of green June beetles.

She tells her students a story about being stopped by a Nazi officer when she was a teenager. The Nazi asked if she was Jewish. "What would you say to a Nazi officer? Quick!" Gerda urges her students. "You can't think long. You have to stay one step ahead of the enemy!"

Hers is not merely a story of survival but of resilience in the face of extinction.

Thank you, Gerda, for sharing your story and so much else with me. It has been a rewarding education, and a reminder that the act of remembering is less about regret than it is about anticipation.

Cecilia Fannon, Editor
February 20, 2019
Laguna Niguel, CA